THE
BRITISH
EMPIRE
IN 100
FACTS

JEM DUDUCU

Dedicated to Liz and the boys, who have learned to live with my love of history

First published 2014

Amberley Publishing
The Hill, Stroud
Gloucestershire, GL5 4EP

www.amberley-books.com

British Library Cataloguing in Publication Data.
A catalogue record for this book is available from the British Library.

ISBN 978 1 4456 4366 3 (paperback)
ISBN 978 1 4456 4399 1 (ebook)

Typeset in 11pt on 13.5pt Sabon.
Typesetting and Origination by Amberley Publishing.
Printed in the UK.

THE FACTS

Introduction

There are some topics in history that are simply massive and the British Empire is one of them. There are dozens of books on the subject, and as the general story has been well covered, the books have become more and more specific, until the subject is a single regiment fighting in an obscure colonial battle. At this point, quite frankly, the casual non-fiction reader has lost interest.

So the purpose of *The British Empire in 100 Facts* is to cover the main trends and themes of the great imperial experiment, as well as to dispel a few myths that continue to swirl around it. The 100 fact format allows for bite-sized history, so you can snack on this information or gorge on it. The choice is yours.

1. THE BRITISH EMPIRE BEGAN IN UNDERWHELMING CIRCUMSTANCES

Possibly the most important thing that happened in the Tudor period was not the ephemeral politics or beheadings, but that in 1497, Humphrey Gilbert became the first European since the time of the Vikings to set foot in North America. This was significant for two reasons:

1. It would eventually lead to the formation of the enormously powerful and globally influential United States of America.
2. It can be seen as the start of the British Empire, which would take another 200 years to reach a critical mass, but would, eventually, become the largest empire in the world.

It was an inauspicious start. Having found this new land, they decided to call it 'Newfoundland', so winning the award for the most literal naming of an area – ever!

In 1607, a group of settlers landed in North America. They founded a small settlement with a defensive fort, which they named Fort James in honour of the king. They called the town Jamestown and the nearest river – go on, guess – the James River. Other settlers did little better. When they tired of naming everything after the king, they named the local area, which reminded them of England, 'New England', thus continuing the underwhelming naming conventions of British explorers.

Unimaginative naming wasn't England's only problem in the New World. Britain was seriously behind in the rush for riches in the Americas. Prior to the Tudor era, France had always been England's chief enemy; however, after 1492 and Christopher Columbus's discovery of the Caribbean islands (spectacularly misnamed the West Indies), the Spanish had 'arrived' in Europe.

Cortez and Pizarro were adventurers who took on entire civilisations. With the latest in weaponry, they had a substantial technological advantage over their Aztec and Incan opponents. They had also created an inadvertent biological weapon by opening up these populations to virulent European diseases to which the conquistadors had natural immunity.

These points help to explain how hundreds of men challenged armies of tens of thousands and won, but they were still tiny bands of adventurers taking on vast empires. They had the right mix of bravery and ruthlessness needed to carve out huge fortunes for themselves and their followers, while shipping similarly colossal amounts of booty back to the motherland.

The South American colonies were built on violence and plunder. This was all ratified by the Pope on the grounds that the locals were godless heathens who carried out human sacrifice. They were. But this is an imperial view of local customs, and although nobody can defend human sacrifice, that didn't justify wholesale slaughter.

The British were fundamentally different in their approach to their American colonies. Let's be honest – this was mainly because there were no easy pickings; these colonies were more about farming, settlement and later, trade. Farmers generally aren't rich, and the ones in America certainly weren't, so these modest starts to empire were initially dwarfed when compared to the Spanish conquests.

2. ENGLAND'S FIRST IMPERIAL FORCE WAS MADE UP OF PIRATES

In the early days of empire, the British Isles were still divided into warring states, and in the meantime, Spain and Portugal had grown enormously wealthy from all the riches stripped from their American colonies. Spain had been particularly lucky in conquering two American empires (Aztecs and Incas), whereas the English, by contrast, had a few tiny outposts scraping a living.

This meant that when it came to warfare between England and Spain, it was always likely to be a Spanish victory ... unless the English got creative. This creativity manifested itself in the emergence of 'the privateer', a captain of a warship that was not part of the Royal Navy. Instead, this captain obtained a 'letter of marque', which was an official government license authorising him to attack and capture a specific country's vessels. It was, in essence, a letter allowing a captain to act like a pirate.

The crew would set off towards areas where they knew they would find trade and transport shipping, and then attack with great vigour. The main focus of attack was the Spanish Main, the coastline of the Spanish territories in America. These covered a vast area from Venezuela, up along the Eastern coast of Mexico, to the peninsula of Florida. The advantage was with the predators because they knew where the targets would be; they would strike quickly and then disappear over the horizon. Any booty would be taken to the safety of an English port, from where it made its way to an 'admiralty court'. Here the plunder would be sold at fixed prices. This not only boosted the coffers of the English government, but also made the privateers rich.

Privateers were seen as both glamorous and patriotic because the plucky underdog was inflicting losses on the great fleets of Spain or Portugal. And since the risks were shared, the crew all got a cut. It was a lucrative business.

By Queen Elizabeth I's rule, privateers were so rife that Spain formally complained on a number of occasions, pointing out (not unreasonably) that their legitimate shipping was being attacked by pirates who were being protected by the English Crown. Elizabeth could, however, always deny that they were her ships or her orders because privateers were not part of the Royal Navy. The technicalities fooled no one.

When the Spanish went to war with Elizabeth, much was made, then and now, of the Catholic versus Protestant angle. The reality is that privateers were as much a cause for war between the two nations as any religious motivation.

Later monarchs like James I and Charles I wanted better relations with Spain, so privateering was curtailed. By the time of the English Civil War, the idea of fighting for profit didn't really fit the puritan ideas of Oliver Cromwell. The era of privateers officially came to an end in 1856, when most major maritime powers signed 'The Paris Declaration Respecting Maritime Law', which abolished the practise.

3. Imperial Invention No. 1: The Flushable Toilet

Britain has given the world many inventions that have improved humanity's lot in life. Throughout this book there will be occasional facts that discuss some of the lesser-known ones.

The first is also one of the most important. Toilets with water systems date back to some ancient civilisations, but the first flushable toilet was invented by Sir John Harington. He installed it in his home in Kelston, Somerset, in the 1590s. He named it Ajax and even wrote a book about it. This last fact may seem surprising, but as well as being a practical and imaginative sort of man, Sir Harington was also a courtier to Queen Elizabeth I, and he had strong political views. In his book entitled *A New Discourse upon a Stale Subject: The Metamorphosis of Ajax*, he used the flushing away of waste as an analogy for the political situation in Britain. Even though his book was written under a pseudonym, he was found out and exiled from court.

He did, however, get back into the queen's good books by installing his new invention for her at Richmond Palace. The queen, while intrigued by this cutting edge sanitation, refused to use it because it made too much noise. Sir Harington's 'Ajax' was not widely adopted in England, but his system did gain popularity in France under the name 'Angrez'.

That's probably all that anyone needs to know on that subject.

4. Sir Francis Drake Was a Slaver, Pirate, Explorer and Hero

Sir Francis Drake was the very embodiment of the attitudes of sixteenth-century England.

During the 1550s, Drake was involved in one of the English raids in Sub-Saharan Africa to capture slaves. Whether he joined for the adventure or purely to capitalise on this profitable business, there is no denying that he made money from the slave trade.

Ferdinand Magellan's expedition may have been the first to circumnavigate the world (although Magellan himself died during the voyage), but Drake was second and made it back alive. During his voyage he did some privateering, preying on the various Spanish ports of South America. His trip took him up the North American coast, across the Pacific, on to Indonesia and then up the West African Coast. It was a journey of truly epic (and extremely lucrative) proportions. He had gathered so much wealth from Spanish gold and rare spices that Queen Elizabeth's cut of the booty amounted to more than her country's annual tax returns!

Most men would have been satisfied with that, but Drake was greedy for more. He went on to become the mayor of Plymouth in 1581 and later became a Member of Parliament.

However, the perennial problem of Spain loomed, and in 1587, Drake led a surprise attack on the Spanish fleet based in Cadiz and Corunna. This time he was not a privateer but an admiral, who led the Royal Navy into battle. He destroyed thirty-seven naval and merchant ships, thus postponing Spanish plans to invade England by a whole year. But this only delayed the inevitable, and in 1588, Philip II of Spain sent an armada to link up with his troops in the Netherlands, from where they began the intended invasion of England. It was Drake who organised the fire ships (stripped down warships full of combustible materials, chained together) that caused the closely packed formation of the Spanish fleet to break up and be defeated by the smaller English force. It was said that Drake 'singed the beard of the King of Spain'. This was Drake's, and therefore Queen Elizabeth's, greatest victory.

By now Drake was in his late forties, hugely wealthy and as well respected as a man could be. It was time to retire, except that Drake just couldn't do it. He returned to the Spanish Main where he raided, plundered and attacked, but the 1590s were not a successful decade for Drake.

Adventure, battles and the high seas are a young man's game, and it was surprising that Drake didn't fall in battle. But with the unsanitary conditions on board Tudor ships in the tropics, he simply fell ill. Dysentery claimed Drake's life, and as he lay dying, he asked to be put in his full armour. He was buried at sea in a lead coffin, near Portobello, Panama. The site of his body has been much sought after but never found.

5. THE PILGRIM FATHERS DIDN'T LEAVE ENGLAND BECAUSE OF PERSECUTION

Once Henry VIII set up the Church of England, some thought he hadn't gone far enough. This new church still had priests and large places of worship full of gold, in many ways resembling the Roman Catholic Church which had just been abolished. The Puritans, as the name suggests, wanted to go further. They wanted to strip away all of the symbols of an organised and hierarchical church and take all the sin and debauchery out of society. It's hard not to consider them miserable spoilsports, but they were on a mission from God; they were doing it for the greater good of the soul. Surely it was better to go to heaven than to be distracted by something as worldly as bawdy Jacobean plays?

The Pilgrim Fathers, who had gone off to start key colonies in America, had not gone because of religious persecution in the way we assume. Because they were so puritanical, they had few sympathisers and received no official backing in England, so they left for the New World where they could do things their way. This combination of genuine religious zeal and an inability to compromise can be seen in some Christian communities in America to this day.

These puritan settlers were so concerned with God's work that they took more Bibles than farming equipment when they went to the New World (and bizarrely, one man took over 100 pairs of shoes), believing that God would provide. However, it is also in the Bible that God helps those who help themselves, and had it not been for the kindness and pity of the local Native Americans, the community would have perished in its first year. These are the origins of the

American Thanksgiving holiday. The first documented Thanksgiving services in territory currently belonging to the United States were conducted by the Spaniards in the sixteenth century. Thanksgiving services were routine in what was to become the Commonwealth of Virginia as early as 1607. The Puritans, being Puritans, repaid the kindnesses of the local natives by declaring them heathens and did their best to steal their land by attacking them with the other thing they had brought plenty of – guns.

The Pilgrims had intended to create 'a new holy land' on the American continent. Their trials and tribulations in these remote settlements were often equated to the hardships the tribes of Israel had faced in the Old Testament. Standards of behaviour were exacting and breaches were severely punished. It didn't take long for the settlers to turn inwards, accusing each other of heresy and witchcraft. In the 1690s, this outbreak of paranoia resulted in the Salem Witch Trials, when dozens of innocent people were convicted of witchcraft and executed. Given their early history of bickering and maladministration, it's a miracle the American colonies endured. America in its infancy very nearly died in the cradle.

6. An English Empire Became a British One, Thanks to Financial Disaster

An event that super-fuelled the rise of the British Empire was actually a national disaster for Scotland, and it was called the Darien Scheme. By the 1690s, the Scottish gentry, businessmen and government all wanted to get on the bandwagon of empire building. For nearly a century, ever since James I/VI had become king after Queen Elizabeth I had died with no children, the crowns of Scotland and England had been joined, but in all other respects, the countries had been separate. They even went to war with one another, although not with the same frequency as before the unification.

While England looked on wistfully at the larger empires of the Spanish, Portuguese and even the Dutch, the Scots were well behind even the English. So Scotland pulled all its resources together in an attempt at a great imperial endeavour. The Scots needed to pick a centre for this lofty undertaking, and they chose an area of modern day Panama, which they named New Caledonia (showing that the Scots were no more original in naming things than the English). It was not an unreasonable idea. By the time the European powers had finished building overseas empires in the nineteenth century, even Belgium had a slice of the pie. Why shouldn't Scotland have its own empire?

However, New Caledonia was a disaster. The area chosen was little more than a malarial swamp. The settlers were ravaged by tropical diseases, which annihilated the population and turned the flood of new arrivals into a trickle. When the Spanish attacked to finish off this potential competitor, they needn't have bothered.

Scotland had badly overexposed itself in this venture, and the state and most of the gentry faced bankruptcy. There wasn't enough money in Scotland to allow the economy to recover. The financial institutions had ground to a halt; the country had undone itself economically.

Because the crowns of Scotland and England were unified, Queen Anne had a vested interest in using the growing financial power of England to aid Scotland. England paid Scotland's bills, and in return, in 1707, the Acts of Union brought together these two old enemies into one unified kingdom.

An emotive way to describe this is a hostile takeover, but Scotland had got itself into its own mess. This new situation, which initially started so cautiously, ended up being a golden opportunity for Scottish entrepreneurs. At a stroke they now had access to all of the colonial markets, with the same rights of trade as the English. From bust, Scotland boomed. Thanks to imperial trade, the tiny town of Glasgow turned into the largest city in the country, just one example of the benefits of union to the Scots. There were also advantages for England: no longer would the country have to keep one eye on a long-contested border; now the two nations could put all their efforts into building a global empire.

7. THE GREATEST GENERAL IN BRITISH HISTORY IS CHURCHILL … JOHN CHURCHILL

The Union of England and Scotland roughly coincided with the struggle for the Spanish throne after King Charles II (of Spain) died in 1700. The subsequent contest became known as the War of the Spanish Succession, when, for over a decade, the kingdoms of Europe created alliances and jockeyed for positions of power. Britain, under Queen Anne, was part of this, and it was she who resurrected the career of an obscure noble and minor military leader, John Churchill.

Although the origins of this conflict were in Spain, Churchill spent his time fighting in Central Europe, allied with the Dutch and various German powers against France (it's a long story). Churchill understood that most vital but often overlooked area of military organisation: logistics. Troops win wars, but well-equipped, well-fed and rested troops, who are paid on time, are more likely to fight hard than ones who aren't. Churchill ensured that as much effort was put into ordnance and provisions as the tactics for any given battle.

This care for supplies was given a physical embodiment when he invented a two-wheeled, lightweight cart with basic suspension, which allowed the army to move quicker. This may not sound like much until it is realised that everyone else was using four-wheeled, heavyweight carts, which were not only hideously slow, but had to travel on existing roads. Churchill's two-wheelers allowed a rapid flanking movement.

But to win the title of 'greatest general', you have to win battles. One of Churchill's earliest turned out to be one of his most famous. The larger French and

Bavarian force assumed Churchill wouldn't attack a strong defensive position. So early on the morning of 13 August 1704, when he led his allied army forwards, he caught the Franco-Bavarian forces by surprise. The British attackers of the pivotal village of Blenheim (hence the name of the battle) were ordered not to fire until they were assaulting the town itself. This prevented any delays in firing and reloading the painfully slow muskets of the age. Speed was of the essence, in Churchill's mind, even if it meant his men were under heavy fire from fixed positions. The press from the allies broke the will of the French and Bavarians, and they began to retreat. In the confusion, French Marshal Tallard was captured. The retreat turned into a rout, and hundreds (if not thousands) of French and Bavarian troops drowned in the Danube as they tried to escape.

This was by no means Churchill's only major victory: there was Ramillies in 1706 and Oudenaarde in 1708, among many others. John Churchill, for his exceptional services to Queen Anne, was made the first Duke of Marlborough, and Blenheim Palace was built for his retirement. He was to fall in and out of favour over time, but he was an exceptional military commander and should be a name better known in Britain.

8. THE EAST INDIA COMPANY WAS ITS OWN EMPIRE

When the early period of the empire is discussed, it largely covers activity in North America, and while it is generally known that Britain had dominions in India, it is not generally known how old they were.

For centuries Indian assets were not technically held by the crown, but by a company. This company was created on New Year's Eve 1600, when Queen Elizabeth I granted a Royal Charter to George, Earl of Cumberland, under the name Governor and Company of Merchants of London trading with the East Indies. This initial enterprise became known as the East India Company.

As the name suggests, the purpose of this organisation was to trade with the East Indies. In the early seventeenth century, places like Indonesia and Malaya were producing spices that could earn a merchant a fortune back in Europe. This is how the Dutch had built their empire – through the Dutch East India Company. However, because the English came late to the spice trade, the British version ended up trading mainly with the Indian sub-continent and China.

In 1608, the East India Company established a settlement at Surat in India, and this became the site of the company's first headquarters. Companies were different to lands owned by the crown because they were driven by market forces. An incompetent noble could end up being governor of Virginia if he had the right connections. However, to rise to a position of importance in the East India Company, you had to be able to do the job. It also explains why the East India Company, time and time again, was able to outmanoeuvre the French, who relied on appointing governors and local rulers with aristocratic connections, rather than appointing those who had shown themselves to be capable of doing what the job demanded. However, having a country ruled by the need for profit, rather than other commercial or national demands, can also get you into serious trouble, as we shall later see.

The initial settlement in Surat was quickly followed, in 1611, by the establishment of a permanent base of trade at Machilipatnam, and a year later, they joined other already established European trading companies in Bengal. This shows the speed at which the company intended to grow. Later, when it was floated on the stock market, it was possible to witness the fluctuations in share price over the eighteenth and nineteenth centuries. The company was a miniature empire in all but name: it had its own army, navy, taxes and hierarchy.

The separation between the crown and the East India Company was, at times, a little murky. For example, Charles II, in 1661, as part of the dowry for marrying Catherine of Braganza, received Bombay from the Portuguese (most people bring crockery to a wedding). However, this was, in turn, given to the East India Company, but was held in trust for the crown (guess he wanted the crockery instead).

9. BRITAIN BUILT AN EMPIRE WITH WORSE WEAPONS THAN THEIR MEDIEVAL COUNTERPARTS

The period of the British Empire roughly covers the era of gunpowder. From the time of John Churchill to the very end of the nineteenth century, red-jacketed forces blasted away with their muskets, from India to Ireland.

However, it's worth pausing to consider why nobody was using longbows. This may sound ridiculous until the advantages of this older weapon are understood. A musket was wildly inaccurate and unlikely to hit anything further away than 100 yards, while the longbow could kill at a quarter of a mile. A musket could fire four to five shots in two minutes, while the longbow could fire forty arrows in the same time. A matchlock musket can't fire in the rain, while a longbow can.

Firearm technology didn't surpass the effectiveness of the longbow until the late nineteenth century. So, putting all this together, it's somewhat surprising that the longbow was abandoned.

The reasons for this are twofold: firstly, it's cheaper and quicker to train someone to fire a tube of gunpowder than it is to train for years to acquire the strength to pull a longbow back to full draw.

Secondly, although the killing power of a longbow isn't in any doubt, there is plenty of evidence that humans would rather not kill each other, so bangs and flashes of flame are very good techniques to scare the enemy away. That way, everyone gets to live to fight another day.

10. The Royal Navy Owes Much to Oliver Cromwell

With the age of empire starting officially in 1497, it is surprising that some traditionalists push the founding of the Royal Navy back to more than 500 years earlier.

The ninth century was a time of Viking invasion. After they were held back by King Alfred the Great, he founded a permanent navy in an attempt to thwart further Viking invasions before they ever reached England.

While all of this is true, it's a bit of a stretch to say the Royal Navy is an Anglo-Saxon invention. The issue here is not one of technology, but more a case of the sporadic nature of navies: sometimes it was just too expensive to maintain them, especially if they were not needed. It is more practical to look for the foundations of the Royal Navy during the reign of Henry VIII. It was under him that the navy got its own dockyards and a stable core of purpose-built warships.

This is the point at which we start to see a permanent administration, ensuring supplies, repairs and what we would recognise as the bare bones of a modern military establishment.

However, it wasn't a king who turned the Royal Navy into a world-beating implement of imperial power, but Oliver Cromwell. With pretty much everyone set against the new English republic, Cromwell needed a strong navy to survive. To symbolise this, his new naval flagship was named the *Naseby* after one of Cromwell's victories.

Ironically, differences over matters of trade led to war with the only other Protestant republic in Europe – the Netherlands. In 1652, the First Anglo-Dutch

War (there were to be three) broke out. The Dutch had a longer tradition of being a seafaring nation and they had some great admirals to lead their fleets; however, that didn't stop the improved Royal Navy from crushing the Dutch in battles at Scheveningen and Portland. The war eventually led to a victory for Cromwell and gave him the breathing space his fledgling republic so desperately needed. This conflict was the first maritime war fought largely by purpose-built, state-owned warships. It was a very different state of affairs from the time of King Alfred.

Ultimately, up until the seventeenth century, England (and later Britain) was just one of many maritime powers, but it was in this century that the Royal Navy learned the lessons of other larger and better funded navies. After this, it never looked back. There would be plenty more naval battles over the next 150 years or so, but by the early nineteenth century, no country or empire on the planet could match the wide-ranging power of the Royal Navy.

Thanks to its cavalry, the Mongol Empire was the largest land-based empire in history – and the second largest overall. Britain had a sea-based empire, making it the largest ever in history, but it couldn't have held together without the might of the Royal Navy.

11. Sir Isaac Newton Was Easily Distracted from His Scientific Work

Sir Isaac Newton was the man who built the first practical reflecting telescope and proved that prisms did not colour light, but split white light into its component colours. He was the man who, with one theory of gravity, could explain how the planets move around the solar system. He laid the foundations for calculus (although Leibnitz would debate that).

Newton's second law declares that 'for every action there is an equal and opposite reaction', which is one of the most famous quotes in science.

The man is simply a giant in scientific and mathematical history, but in reality he spent quite a lot of time not being a scientist.

Newton was an odd guy – singe minded, egotistical and arrogant (undeniably, he had much to be arrogant about). He wrote his famous book, *Principia Mathematica*, in Latin to make it deliberately hard to read in order to keep the riff-raff away from his coveted theories. He nearly blinded himself twice, once by staring at the sun through a telescope (he had to stay in a darkened room for days to recover). On the other occasion he tried to place a needle behind his eyeball. Again, he didn't cause himself any permanent damage.

Perhaps most frustratingly for everyone, he would spend years coming up with ideas and formulae and then fail to record them in any useful or meaningful way. It was not unusual for scraps of paper to be discarded, found and then lost again.

For about half of his academic life, Newton didn't pursue mainstream science at all. He was obsessed with alchemy. Alchemy is often thought to be about turning base metals into gold, but another potential prize is the fabled 'philosopher's stone', the formula for immortality. It's hard to think that someone as smart as Newton could be distracted by the idea of magic potions (he seemed to think metals were somehow alive), but it could be that he also thought he had the brain to crack this legendary challenge. Ultimately, it meant many years exploring a dead end of chemistry.

For many years Newton worked for the Royal Mint, eventually becoming the Master of the Mint. Even though forging coins was a criminal act which sometimes resulted in the death penalty, Newton seemed a little too obsessed with prosecuting forgers. He estimated that about 20 per cent of the realm's coinage was counterfeit, and he was determined to see the perpetrators pay. He went undercover, gathered much of the evidence himself, and in just one year (when he also acted as the prosecution) had twenty-eight counterfeiters convicted. One man, William Chaloner, was a career conman and counterfeiter. Newton badly wanted to get him but failed in the first instance, so he gathered enough evidence for a second attempt, this time on a charge of high treason. Newton's prosecution was successful and Chaloner was sentenced to be hung, drawn and quartered.

Sir Isaac Newton: genius scientist, but not a nice man.

12. THE FIRST STEAM ENGINE DIDN'T MOVE

Using steam to create movement or to induce a mechanism to turn or engage has been around since the time of the Ancient Greeks. But even then it was regarded as a fanciful notion and was forgotten in the medieval and renaissance eras.

The idea was to remain dormant for many centuries until it was resurrected by a most unlikely candidate. Thomas Newcomen was a Baptist lay preacher, but he also ran an ironmonger, which specialised in mining equipment.

In those days the risk of flooding in deep mines was an ever present danger, so Newcomen devised a mechanical pump. Not content with this, between the years of 1710–1712, he went on to invent a steam-powered pump. This was the world's first steam-powered device to produce mechanical work, which is technically all a machine has to do to be considered a 'steam engine'.

The machine was extremely inefficient, losing most of its power through escaping heat and steam, but it was a start. (It would take more than sixty years for the famous James Watt to create his much improved version of the Newcomen engine.) It greatly reduced the work needed to avoid flooding in mines. It also can be regarded as the point at which man decided that he should start travelling faster than horses.

So, it can be said that the industrial revolution started with a Baptist minister who had an ironmonger business.

13. General George Monck Stopped a War

The way to get noticed as a military leader is to carry out some daring tactic that efficiently defeats the enemy. It must be said that on the rare occasion when a leader so completely outmanoeuvres the opposition that there is no war, he is usually not that well remembered. Surely a victory with no blood spilt is the best kind of victory?

General George Monck is one such unique military leader. During the English Civil War and later, under the republic, Monck was an officer on both sides, so he was well placed to see the situation from all viewpoints. Once Cromwell died, his son Richard was put in charge, but that didn't work out.

Many people wanted the monarchy back, but not the absolute monarchy that King Charles I had tried to impose. Between the winter of 1658 and the summer of 1660, anything could have happened. The most likely outcome was a third round of civil war. Monck, however, managed to outmanoeuvre everyone who could have vied for power and, without firing a shot, positioned himself as the *de facto* power in the land. He did this by careful political manipulation, ensuring no party was painted into a corner. If nobody felt an existential threat, then everyone could behave honourably. He also, literally, marched his forces around Scotland and England, using his authority and reputation, not to engage enemy troops, but to disband them. Once he had arrived in London with his army, he invited Charles I's son and heir to come home and restore the monarchy.

The people of the British Isles were exhausted from

war and wanted no more. Monck performed a service for everyone and deserved both recognition and thanks for selflessly handing over the reins of power to a monarch who could unite the country. A powerful general, with an army in the capital city and a navy at his command ... and he handed all of this over to an exile. How often do you read about that?

The Declaration of Breda, which was designed to reconcile and forgive the monarchy, was based on many of Monck's notions of giving all sides some face-saving measures. Monck disbanded the New Model Army (although his regiment, the Coldstream Guards, remains to this day) and was lavishly rewarded after the Restoration. He was given lands and titles and became a Knight of the Garter, with an annual pension of £7,000 (a huge amount for the time).

Fortunately, Charles II was a very different ruler. He was the 'Merry Monarch' who brought back theatre and initiated scientific endeavours such as the Royal Society and the Royal Observatory in Greenwich. Monck's gamble paid off and played a significant part in ensuring the young empire didn't keep tearing itself to pieces.

General George Monck is a man largely forgotten by history, but his name should be remembered, and with gratitude. It's not often that a general stops wars and saves lives.

14. Nature Abhors a Vacuum: After the Plague, a New Pathogen Starts

The Black Death arrived in Britain in 1348, long before the start of the British Empire, but it didn't entirely leave for centuries. Every now and then, outbreaks of the plague would burst forth, spread like wildfire and kill thousands.

Edward III was king in 1348, but more than 300 years later, Charles II still had to worry about it. The sickness was usually caused by bubonic plague, spread by the *Yersinia pestis* bacterium, which would breed in the gut of fleas that lived on rats. When these fleas bit humans, the pathogen was passed on. While this chain of infections and events are known now, such understandings were beyond the science of the time. None of this was helped by the fact that the plague seems also to have occasionally mixed with the airborne pneumonic plague, meaning no rats were needed. However, even then, rats were never seen as a good thing, and London had rat catchers who were forever trying to keep the vermin population in check.

When the plague struck again in 1665, it was to be remembered as the Great Plague. The royal court was forced to leave London and relocate to Oxford. Records from the time show that plague deaths in London (and its suburbs) grew inexorably from a summer average of 2,000 deaths per week, to an eventual peak of over 7,000 per week in September.

What ultimately stopped it, once and for all, was the Great Fire of London in early September 1666 (London had a really bad twelve months that year). The fire had been an accident, but with 13,000 homes destroyed, people wanted someone to blame. That someone happened to be a French watchmaker called Robert Hubert, who was hanged for 'admitting' to starting the fire. He was framed, but executing him made everyone feel better (apart from Robert).

However, following the fire, the great affliction of plague, which had lasted for centuries in Britain, was never to return. It seems all vestiges of the pathogen had been destroyed in the fire. It was also sheer good luck that further outbreaks in other countries never managed to make their way into the ports on England's south coast.

As the saying goes, nature abhors a vacuum. So another disease that had been ravaging Asia for millennia became the new lethal illness in Britain – smallpox. Although it had existed prior to the 1660s, it was never commented on with anything like the fear or frequency as the plague. It would be another 140 years before a British scientist would come up with a way to thwart that virus. Until then, this highly infectious and routinely fatal illness would cast its shadow over Britain. It was such a disfiguring disease that survivors would often be left with pox marks, forever literally marking them out and making them near outcasts in society.

15. THE BRITISH EMPIRE HAD SURPRISINGLY FEW EMPERORS

In the year 1707, the Russian Empire had a tsar, the Ottoman Empire had a sultan, and the Holy Roman Empire in Germany had a holy roman emperor. Empires have emperors, it's kind of the rule, and yet the newly created union between Scotland and England meant that the now rebranded 'British' Empire was headed up by Queen Anne, a title that monarchs in Great Britain had been using prior to union, prior to empire and now, with the advent of empire. Why did subsequent British monarchs not become emperors? We have to go back to Oliver Cromwell to explain this.

In essence, the English Civil War tipped the balance of power. Prior to this, the monarch had ultimate authority; afterwards, Parliament had it. When Charles II was allowed back into the country, he had no intention of having his head removed, so he was not going to argue long and hard about who had the ultimate power. The reign of William and Mary further showed that real power wasn't held by the monarchy, but by the political administration around it.

The situation gave Britain an advantage. With an absolute monarchy, government is only as good as its ruler. Sometimes you get a Louis XIV or a Peter the Great, but sometimes you get complete incompetents, like Louis XVI. However, if it's the machinery of government doing the hard work, then there's a level of consistency and stability, which Britain had found by accident.

Queen Anne tried her best to produce an heir for the throne. She was pregnant nineteen times, but none of her children made it to adulthood. The efforts ravaged her body, and she died before her time. In a way, she needn't have bothered. The country was now run by Parliament, not the monarch. After her death, the British government searched Europe for a suitable new sovereign. They wanted a European Protestant royal vaguely related to previous British monarchs. They came up with George of Hanover. He couldn't speak English and wasn't British in any discernible way. Although this slim claim to the throne a hundred years earlier might have led to civil war, by the eighteenth century, it was actually a strength. It allowed the government to get on with running the country and a burgeoning empire, while George I got on with living in palaces.

This state of affairs led to Robert Walpole becoming Britain's first prime minister in 1721. For twenty years, Walpole busied himself with the job of governing. Unlike the rest of Europe, Britain now had an effective bureaucracy that could run independently of the whims of the monarch. This allowed for a continuity of effective governance that other countries wouldn't have for a century or so.

16. George I Didn't Bring His Wife to Britain

George I never brought his wife to England, but there was a very good reason for this.

George was a strange choice for King of England: he wasn't English, there were over fifty nobles with better claims to the throne (but they were Catholic), he was no great statesman and he was a divorcee. It's this last fact that introduces Sophia Dorothea of Celle, who could have been Queen of England, but never was.

Sophia had strong links to the new Hanoverian dynasty: as well as being the wife of George I, she was also his cousin (not cool) and the mother of George II. With a wealthy and impeccable noble lineage, Sophia had the potential to marry into any number of dynasties (she nearly married the King of Denmark); however, when she was sixteen and it was announced that she was to marry her cousin, she famously remarked, 'I will not marry the pig snout!' and threw a miniature of George against the wall. The omens for a happy marriage were not good.

The motivation for the union was financial. George, as Elector of Hanover, was wealthy, as was his cousin; marriage would unite the family fortunes, and in the words of George's own mother, 'One hundred thousand thalers a year is a goodly sum to pocket, without speaking of a pretty wife, who will find a match in my son George Louis, the most pig-headed, stubborn boy who ever lived, who has round his brains such a thick crust that I defy any man or woman ever to discover what is in them.' And that's the view of his own mother! Nobody much liked George.

After the births of their first two children, George

became ever increasingly distracted by his mistress, the rather stout Duchess of Kendal and Munster. It's hardly surprising then that Sophia also had an affair, in her case, with a Swedish count. When the affair was discovered, the count was packed off to war in order to keep the lovers apart. The count returned, however, and had a rendezvous with Sophia at Leineschloss Castle, after which he disappeared, apparently murdered on the orders of a jealous (and hypocritical) George.

When George confronted Sophia about the affair, the conversation turned into an argument, which escalated to the point where George physically attacked Sophia. He pulled and tore out some of her hair and then leapt on her in an attempt to strangle her. His assault was so vicious that he left bruises on her neck. Sophia was saved when her attendants forcibly dragged the incensed George away (ladies and gentlemen, I give you the behaviour of a future King of Great Britain). It probably comes as no surprise that after this incident, Sophia was divorced by her husband, who then had her imprisoned in the Castle of Ahlden. She remained in captivity until her death, more than thirty years later.

17. The Early Eighteenth Century Was the Era of the Wig

The wig has been significant in many eras of history. The images of ancient Egyptian pharaohs with their lush heads of hair are actually images with wigs. The Romans, too, used them, but they eventually fell out of fashion.

That lasted until people (including the aristocracy) started shaving their heads to get rid of the ever-present head lice. The simplest way to cover up a bald head? Use a wig and, rather than having something that looked natural, why not wear something that enhances your splendour? This new wave of wigs was known as 'periwigs' by contemporaries. When powerful monarchs like Charles II, Queen Elizabeth I and Louis XIV took to them, the wig was back in a big way.

The fact that wigs found favour with the rich and powerful meant that wig makers became important people, and the first wig makers' guild was established in France in 1665. While the cheapest wigs were made of horse hair, the very finest were made of human hair.

The wigs of the seventeenth century were usually natural in colour; it wasn't until the eighteenth century that wig fashion really got out of hand. Special powders were used to make the wigs appear either grey or light blue, and they were often fragranced. Wigs were considered to be not only acceptable for men, but *de rigueur* in the upper echelons of society. They were even worn into battle. John Churchill and, later, the officers of the British army fighting in the Seven Years' War and the American Revolution not only had to deal with life and death decisions, they had to do this with itchy wigs on their heads.

Wigs were warm and uncomfortable in the best of circumstances, so you have to wonder at the resolve of European officers who wore these in the heat of the tropics, simply to remain fashionable. Fainting was frequent at colonial dinner parties.

The women got off lighter in the wig department. Most ladies tended not to wear wigs, but they did have hair extensions which were often scooped up and turned into elaborate hair styles that were, literally, stacked on top of the woman's head.

Two very different events led to the demise of the wig. Thanks to the French Revolution in 1789, the wig became a symbol of aristocratic decadence (they had a point) and the wearing of them was abolished (it was also illegal for women in France to wear trousers, a law that went unnoticed until its quiet retirement in 2014).

The other reason was far more mundane. In 1795 the British government introduced a tax on hair powder. The cost was one guinea a year, which was high price to pay for fashion. This tax led to the rapid decline of both the fashion for wigs and powder. Indeed, just a generation later, during the Napoleonic wars, nobody in that war wore wigs.

18. 'Black Bart' Roberts Personified the Golden Age of Piracy

From roughly 1700 to 1730 the Atlantic, Indian and Caribbean waters were home to a common predator – pirates.

After the War of the Spanish Succession (remember John Churchill), there were thousands of idle, well-trained sailors floating around the seven seas, looking for an opportunity. Many spotted their chance in piracy. Pirates were greedy, but they weren't stupid and for very good reasons: they were selective about their targets. Since some colonial ports were richer than others, why not concentrate on the richer prizes? But apart from plunder potential, security and geography were also factors. The commercial ships sailing the vast Indian Ocean were laden with exotic spices, silks and other treasures. With few warships to protect them, why not prey on easy pickings?

The very best pirates are unknown to history; they had a few successes and melted away to enjoy their ill-gotten gains. Famous pirates, like Captain Kidd and Blackbeard, were only active for a handful of years before being caught and executed. Perhaps the most infamous pirate of the period was Bartholomew 'Black Bart' Roberts. His story is typical of the pirates of the era.

His first act was meant to avenge the death of his old captain, who had just been killed on the island of Principe (a Portuguese colony off the west coast of Africa). Roberts and his men returned to kill the governor (and a large proportion of the men on the island), stole what they could and, days after leaving the scene of the crime, managed to capture two ships, one Dutch and one British. Not bad for a first raid.

Black Bart's voyages show the range of piracy. In 1720 he headed over to Brazil for more successful raiding and then sailed up to Canada. These are vast stretches of ocean which only skilled sailors could successfully navigate, and as if to prove the point, in 1721 Roberts moved back to the west coast of Africa to attack French shipping. During the course of his career, Black Bart captured over 400 vessels.

In 1722 he was ashore at Cape Lopez (in Gabon), carousing with some of his crew (the so-called 'pirate code' was surprisingly strict regarding life on board: no gambling, women or drunkenness), when he realised an approaching ship was not a merchant vessel, but the HMS *Swallow*. He rallied his (still drunk) crew and quickly boarded his own ship, where he calculated that he would have to survive one broadside from the *Swallow*'s cannons before he could slip past and escape. As the *Swallow*'s broadside did not cause too much damage, Black Bart's luck held. However, because the crew was still sozzled, they didn't clear the Royal Navy ship fast enough, giving the *Swallow*'s crew the opportunity for a second volley. This time Black Bart was struck in the throat by canister shot and died. His death is often seen as the end of the golden age of piracy.

19. The Glorious Revolution Sparked the Jacobite Movement

The line of Charles I was a fraught one. He lost his head, while his eldest son lived for years in exile. Charles II also had problems keeping his throne. His eldest illegitimate son, the Duke of Monmouth, invaded England to claim the throne in 1685. It was an atrociously planned uprising, which a young John Churchill helped to suppress. Monmouth was found guilty of treason, resulting in an unexpectedly gruesome execution. The executioner was drunk, and his first swing of the axe was just a glancing blow. It took a further five swings before the business was finished off by an onlooker with a knife.

In the midst of dynastic scheming, the British government rumbled on, but everything came to a peak when Charles's successor, his younger brother James, became king. James lasted three years before he was expelled for his pro-French Catholic attitudes, in favour of his daughter Mary and her Dutch husband. This was the 'Glorious Revolution'.

James was understandably shocked by his enforced retirement. Still believing it was his divine right to rule the British Isles, he moved his court to France, which welcomed him as someone who would happily cause trouble for its oldest enemy.

The followers of James (and later, his descendants) were called 'Jacobites' from Jacobus, the Latin for James. Over the years their central goal (James's right to rule) became mixed with the goals of anti-unionists in Scotland, as well as with those of Catholics who felt victimised by a Protestant-ruled Britain. The first problem for the Jacobites was that James's family was still on the throne. Mary was his daughter, and later, Queen Anne was another of his offspring. Further turmoil was added to an already tense situation after Anne died childless and the Jacobites had a much better claim to the British throne than George of Hanover. This state of affairs could be regarded as extremely unfair to James's eldest and exiled son, James Francis, who was dubbed 'the old pretender' by anti-Jacobites and 'the king over the water' by his Jacobite supporters.

Events culminated in 1715 when James Francis, in association with the Scottish Earl of Mar, raised a highland army and marched into England. The timing was terrible. France had lost the War of the Spanish Succession and had signed a peace treaty with Britain in 1713, so it wasn't going to help the insurrection. Worse, other areas of Britain failed to rise up in support as anticipated. After two battles (a small one at Preston and a much larger one at Sheriffmuir), the rebellion fizzled out. James Francis, who was always nervous with crowds, was not the leader the highlanders had been hoping for, and after the failure of the uprising and the death of Louis XIV, he wasn't welcome back in France. It was the Pope who took pity on him and installed him in a palace in Rome.

20. George II Had Unusual Claims to Fame

George II became king after his father's death in 1727. This George was the last King of England (or Great Britain) to have been born outside the United Kingdom.

However, unlike his father, George II actually liked Britain and could even speak the language. Because his father had not intended that he should get both the British crown and the Hanoverian lands, George II was forced to suppress his father's will, an action which proved to be popular both on the continent and in Britain. His failure to attend his father's funeral in Germany was seen as another sign of his fondness for Britain. He was, however, Hanovarian at heart and spent a dozen summers there during his reign.

The family problems continued with George's son, Frederick, Prince of Wales. Possibly because they had not seen each other for fourteen years, Frederick hated his father, and for decades the Prince of Wales was a rallying figure for opposition to the king. Frederick was regarded as so untrustworthy that when George travelled to the continent, he put his wife in charge of the regency council. When Frederick died in 1751, George finally got some peace and quiet in the last decade of his reign. The new heir to the throne was Frederick's brother George (another one), who also had some interesting issues that will be discussed later.

In 1740, during George II's reign, the War of the Austrian Succession broke out. Like the similar sounding War of the Spanish Succession a generation earlier, this was another horribly complicated European conflagration based on a simple debate over inheritance (in this case, should Maria Theresa be allowed to run Austria?) that led to the deaths of hundreds of thousands of people, on land and at sea (many with their wigs on). Suffice it to say that Britain and France were at war again, each with various other nations as their allies.

In 1743 in Bavaria, British allied forces met the French at the Battle of Dettingen. This fairly obscure engagement involved more than 50,000 troops in total. Its importance was twofold: as well as being a significant allied victory, it was also the last time a monarch of Great Britain led troops into battle. George II's contributions shouldn't be overstated – he was no Henry V and didn't share anything like the danger that front line troops had to face. At one point his horse panicked and charged off the field of battle (a nearby ensign managed to save the king and got a promotion for his trouble). In the future other royals would fight in battles, but before they ascended to the throne.

The war ended in 1748 with very little changed in terms of the political spheres of influence. Only Prussia (which had been on the French side) made any notable gains in territory, and Maria Theresa got to keep Austria. So it was all worth it, then.

21. THE JACOBITES FREED SCOTLAND ... BY ATTACKING ENGLAND

During the War of the Austrian Succession, the Jacobites decided to try again to overthrow the Hanoverians running Britain. Things came to a head in 1745 with James Francis sending his son, Charles Edward Louis John Casimir Sylvester Severino Maria Stuart, to Scotland to head up another Scottish invasion of England (you'll be pleased to know he's remembered as 'Bonnie Prince Charlie', and yes, one of his names was Maria).

Unlike 1715, the timing was much better. Britain was at war with France, so the Jacobites could expect French assistance. Louis XV sent Charles with a small force, munitions and a few small French warships to Scotland. However, on the voyage north, the small fleet was discovered by a Royal Navy squadron, and the ships with the troops and munitions were badly damaged, forcing them back to France. As a result, Charles arrived in the Outer Hebrides pretty much on his own. Needless to say, the expectant Jacobite highlanders were disappointed.

Nevertheless, Charles was a rallying figure, and a small army of 3,000 gathered. As all the best British troops were busy on the continent, Charles and the highlanders had little difficulty beating back British troops, capturing Perth and then Edinburgh. Charles was proclaimed James VIII at Holyrood Palace. It's worth noting that he, not Scotland, held these towns; many Scots regarded Charles as an invader and resented his ambition for an absolute monarchy.

Panic gripped London, a panic that was not relieved when several Jacobite raids on British forces in Scotland in September were also successful. The French sent the Jacobites some supplies and promised an invasion of southern England by the end of the year. This would be a perfect pincer movement, with the Jacobites sweeping down from the north and the French coming in from the south. It was a worst case scenario for George and Parliament.

Charles decided to move things along by saying that the French invasion was imminent. It wasn't and was never going to happen, but the lie spurred the Jacobites to head south, where they got as far as Derby. By this time the English had rallied an army of experienced soldiers under the Duke of Cumberland, and Charles was forced to admit his lie. The Scots retreated in good order, closely followed by Cumberland.

The forces eventually collided at the Battle of Culloden in April 1746, where Charles underestimated what a well-drilled regular army could do after fighting so many militia units. It was a crushing defeat, whereupon Charles immediately abandoned the Scots, blaming treachery (and not his own lack of ability) for defeat.

The Battle of Culloden is significant for two reasons: firstly, it was the last serious threat from the Jacobites, and secondly, it was the last pitched battle fought on British soil. Charles cast around for another chance, but he was either so arrogant or so drunk that he alienated all potential supporters. He died in relative obscurity in 1788.

22. Britain Was Involved in Four World Wars

What makes a war a 'world war'? In the 1914–18 war there was a lot of conflict in Europe, a huge amount in western Russia, some in the Middle East and minor battles in Africa and the Pacific. North America and India sent troops, as did Australia and New Zealand, but the whole of South America and most of Asia was unaffected. So if many countries and at least three continents are required for world war, then Britain has been involved in four.

While it is true that there had been fighting in the colonies of the various imperial powers in the earlier Spanish/Austrian succession wars, they had been little more than skirmishes. In 1756 a much larger conflict broke out, which was to be called the Seven Years' War. It was this war that turned Britain from an imperial power into *the* imperial power of the world.

Britain had the good fortune to ally with the Prussian ruler, Frederick the Great. He was able to hold his own with inferior numbers, fighting on multiple fronts against France, Austria and Russia. His stout resistance meant that Britain could concentrate on fighting in the colonies.

In 1759, following a three-month siege and a sneak attack, General Wolfe was able to capture Quebec from the French. At a stroke, this made Canada British.

In India, impressive gains were made at the expense of the French and their Indian allies. It was this seven-year conflict that enabled British interests in India to become a sub-continent-dominating administration.

The most important naval victory in the Seven Years' War occurred in 1759 at Quiberon Bay. It was the job of Admiral Hawke to stop the planned French invasion of England, which he did by successfully blockading the French navy on its coast near Brest. Hawke had all the motivation he needed as he had succeeded Admiral Byng, who, three years earlier, had failed to relieve Minorca in the first sea battle causing the island to fall into French hands and the British to withdraw to Gibraltar. Byng was tried for 'failing to do his utmost' and was executed by firing squad (an extremely rare punishment). Hawke was determined 'to do his utmost'.

But by November, severe winter weather had set in, and the sea was rough. Hawke, not wanting to risk his fleet, felt forced to retreat. This allowed the French to make a break for it.

As a storm blew up, the French moved their fleet into Quiberon Bay. It was a safe move that should have ensured a stalemate, but Hawke was not going to be accused of over-cautious tactics, and even though he was battling gale force winds, he ordered his fleet to chase the enemy.

The French formation was in disarray, and Hawke made the most of it, attacking what ships he could and causing panic among the remainder. It was a complete fiasco for the French navy, with over a quarter of its fleet destroyed and one ship captured. It was one of Britain's greatest and most technically difficult victories over the French.

23. ROBERT OF INDIA HAD AN UNPROMISING START

As a young man, Robert Clive went to India with his father to work for the East India Company. His duties were largely administrative, and history looked set to pass Clive by. However, in 1746, the First Carnatic (Southern Indian) War broke out, and Clive took the unusual step of enlisting. In 1747 he was recognised for his bravery in the defence of Fort St David and was promoted to ensign. Once peace with France was declared, the East India Company set its sights on Tanjore, and Clive was tasked, with less than 750 men, to assault a fort. The assault was successful (though he was nearly killed), and they achieved an unexpected victory.

Later, in another of the endless wars in India, Clive successfully defended the fort of Arcot. His defence was so vigorous that the event made him famous, and he finished the campaign a hero. Covered in glory, he returned to Britain where he served as an MP for a few years.

Having been made the Deputy Governor of Fort St David at Cuddalore, Clive returned to India in 1755. Shortly afterwards, the Seven Years' War broke out, and Clive was confronted by various enemy Indian princes and French garrisons, ready to take on the East India Company.

In 1757 he was to face his greatest challenge at the Battle of Plassey. It was here that Clive's Anglo-Indian army of just over 3,000 met a Franco-Bengal army of over 60,000. Outgunned and outnumbered twenty to one, defeat seemed inevitable. However, within this formidable army, the Nawab of Bengal had his own divisions. Clive had negotiated an earlier treaty with the nawab, which meant that many of the opposing forces had no plan to attack him.

The French and Bengal cannons started the battle, but after receiving light casualties, Clive retired his troops behind an embankment. The enemy cannons pounded away, ineffectually, for hours. The rest of the battle involved the rapid capture of a strategic French position, followed by more artillery duels. All the Indian cavalry attacks were broken up with canisters of grapeshot (rather than one large cannon ball, this was basically a tin can full of ball bearings, which converted a cannon into a giant shot gun), lethal to both infantry and cavalry. By the end of the day, just twenty-two of his men had been killed, and Bengal capitulated to the East India Company.

Clive fought further battles during the war and remained in India until 1767. His actions made the East India Company (and therefore Britain) the premier power in India. The Mughal Empire, which had once dominated Indian politics (and had been dismissive of the fledgling British company), was now on the defensive and would never recover. This was confirmed in 1760 when a Mughal army, supported by the French, attacked Patna and was defeated by an Anglo-Indian army led by Major John Caillaud. India would remain British for nearly another 200 years.

24. THE BRITISH CAN BE NICE TO THE FRENCH

The end of the Seven Years' War was marked by the signing of the Treaty of Paris in 1763 (twenty years later, there was another Treaty of Paris, which ended the American War of Independence). What seems odd today is that many of the British gains were returned to the defeated countries. This practice was not unusual in European treaties of the eighteenth century.

The idea behind it was that one could keep the neighbours at least mildly satisfied or expect another war, sooner rather than later. As Europe was constantly at war anyway, it was an idea that singularly failed.

But in this instance, Britain didn't want to appear too smug and overbearing to the soundly beaten French. Ironically, France also agreed, but for the completely opposite reason: the French assumed that they would soon again be at war with Britain and expected to make further gains.

A case in point shows the discrepancy between size and value. Guadeloupe is a group of Caribbean islands with a land area of 1,628 km². In the mid-eighteenth century it was one of the biggest sugar producing islands in the world, generating around £6 million worth of sugar each year (today, that's billions). Contrast these small islands with Canada, which is vast and actually cost the crown money to maintain. There was much debate about whether Britain should keep Guadeloupe, the new cash cow, or keep Canada. Both had been captured from the French during the Seven Years' War, but eventually, it was decided that Britain could do with a greater presence in North America. As a result Guadeloupe was (reluctantly) returned to France, but it was due to the consequences of this war that French influence all but disappeared from North America.

While France did not see her overseas empire dissolve because of this give and take, there was no hiding the fact that the country, on this occasion, had come off much worse. Apart from its diminishing interests in the Americas, France was also losing out in India, where the East India Company had taken vital steps to dominate the country. Although France had some face-saving trading posts and warehouses returned, it was forced to recognise British dominion over the whole of Bengal, a massive area (to contrast it with Guadeloupe) of 232,752 km^2 and an area which, unlike Canada, was already turning a profit and had a vast population to support it.

After this hugely successful war (from the British point of view), the Gold State Coach was presented to the king. The coach weighs four tons and must be drawn by eight horses. As any incline makes it too heavy for the horses to pull, it can only go on a flat surface. Because of its weight and the resulting lack of manoeuvrability, it is reserved for important state occasions and has been used at the coronation of every British monarch since George IV.

25. Imperial Invention No. 2: Economics

There is a rather mean cliché about the Scots that they are 'careful' with money. Not only does the Darien Scheme (see Fact 6) prove this wrong, but so does a Fife born man called Adam Smith. In 1776 Smith wrote a revolutionary book with the catchy title *An Inquiry into the Nature and Causes of the Wealth of Nations*. Okay, so he needed to do some work on the title, but the content was electrifying.

For the first time in history, someone was trying to summarise the ebb and flow of money in trade, taxes and business. The amalgamation of these interests is today called 'economics'; and it all started with this one book.

Prior to Smith's book, it was always assumed that in a transaction between a buyer and seller, the buyer *always* lost. Why? Because at the end of the transaction the seller had the money, therefore the seller won. Now the contemporary consumer's logical retort to this is, 'Hang on! The seller may have the money, but the buyer has the goods – and they are also worth something'. This was one of Adam Smith's key ideas, so from this it is possible to see how we have all been influenced by Adam Smith and his theories, theories which are still hotly debated to this day.

Not realising how pervasive his ideas had become, Smith expressed disappointment at the end of his life that he had not achieved more.

26. George Washington Should Have Died Many Times Before He Did

In 1776, when the American colonies rebelled against the mother country, the fate of the rebels rested in the hands of the ex-British Army colonel, George Washington. Although he frequently risked his life fighting for the rebel cause, there were numerous other occasions when Washington could have, or should have, died ... and that's putting aside the high infant mortality rate of the time.

Washington's military career began as a British officer in the Seven Years' War (called the French and Indian War in America). In 1754 he was tasked with defending Fort Necessity in Pennsylvania. The French successfully captured the fort, and the defenders lost a quarter of their number who were killed, wounded or captured. The Anglo-American force was allowed to leave after negotiations, but the lack of discipline on the part of the Native American forces fighting with the French meant that they began looting Washington's men. Incidents like these could lead to a massacre. However, Washington allowed them to take what they wanted – for days – and it never led to bloodshed. Washington got through all of this unharmed.

A year later, he was serving with General Braddock when the Anglo-American force was ambushed by French and Native American forces. Nearly half of the British expeditionary force of 2,100 were either killed or wounded (including Braddock). It was Washington who rallied the troops and got them out of harm's way.

Then, early in the American Revolution, he led the Continental Army at the Battle of Long Island, the largest battle fought during the rebellion. The

Americans were outmanoeuvred and had it not been for the stout resistance of a small detachment of Maryland troops, far more of the army would have been captured. As it was, 20 per cent of the army was lost. The Americans could have been cut off and besieged, but Washington managed to extract the rest of his force under the cover of night. The evacuation took longer than anticipated, and had a fog not come in the following morning, the subterfuge would have been discovered – and again, Washington could have been killed or captured.

The final twist of fate happened the following year on 11 September 1777. A detachment of green-clad British marksmen, led by Captain Patrick Ferguson, one of the best shots in the army, hid in the woods along Brandywine Creek (Pennsylvania again) where he kept a lookout for American forces. When a cavalry officer, dressed in the flamboyant uniform of a European hussar, rode into view, he was followed by a senior American officer wearing a high cocked hat.

The man in the cocked hat had his back to Ferguson, and even though he knew the man was a high value target, Ferguson refused to kill him in such an ungentlemanly fashion. The next day he found out he had had George Washington in his sights.

27. THERE ARE MANY UNREASONABLE REASONS FOR THE AMERICAN REVOLUTION

New England in the 1770s was a hotbed of rebellion, which is odd because the people there were better off than those in Britain. Not only did they have comparable incomes with, generally speaking, more land than the average Brit, but they also paid a lot less tax.

Further, the British government *did* listen to its American colonials. In 1765 the Stamp Act put a tax on paper; it was hugely unpopular, so the tax was withdrawn (and a minister resigned). Next there was a tax on external trade, which was also withdrawn. After that the only tax left on trade in America was the one on tea. So in 1773, when Boston had its 'Tea Party' (actually a riot which destroyed private property), it was against a background of decreasing, not increasing, taxation.

The revolutionary zealots all had their own personal reasons to feel aggrieved. Paul Revere had lost his silversmith business because of the downturn in trade during the Seven Years' War. Samuel Adams had had a few failed businesses, and as an ex-tax collector, he had something of an obsession with taxation. But the colonists were hardly suppressed or overtaxed.

Slightly earlier in 1770, there had been the so-called 'Boston Massacre'. When eight British soldiers were being threatened and having bottles and stones thrown at them, they opened fire (with no orders to do so) and killed five of the mob. The incident was turned into a propaganda coup by the revolutionaries, but the troops were successfully defended in court by John Adams (who was later the second president of the

United States). The event had been an unfortunate one, but it was not a sign of military heavy handedness.

In response to all of this, the prime minister (who, unusually, was also the Chancellor of the Exchequer), Lord North, sent in troops to maintain calm, but in the circumstances, North was too heavy handed, and the troops were turned into pariahs just for being there (memories of the 'massacre' were still fresh in the minds of the New Englanders). However, there was no martial law, civilians were not rounded up and no revolutionary was tried for sedition or treason.

Instead, Britain tried to calm the situation by deploying troops in Boston and introducing some punitive laws, rather than using actual force. These new laws were referred to collectively as the Intolerable Acts. The law that really annoyed the revolutionaries was the one that enlarged the boundaries in the Province of Quebec, designed purely to stop the westward spread of the American colonies.

Therefore, unlike almost any other revolution in history, the American colonists had very few genuine grievances. The imperial power was not crushing the local population. The average citizen was both prosperous and had prospects. There was a cultural and ethnic affinity with the mother country. Things weren't perfect, but this really was the most petulant revolution in history.

28. THE FRENCH WON THE AMERICAN REVOLUTION

Certain aspects of the American Revolution are often misrepresented by traditional folklore. One popular image is that of red-jacketed Brits blundering around the forests of North America, easy targets for the brave American militia. Ambushes happened, but not that often, and the Continental Army did fight pitched battles, but often lost. Indeed, these events led John Adams to wryly observe, 'In general our generals are out generalled.' The reality was that many fighting on the 'American' side still felt an affinity to the mother country, often because they had been born there. Similarly, the British Army had thousands of colonists fighting on its side. Not everyone was happy with the war's outcome, and it was estimated that more than 100,000 colonists moved to Canada just to remain part of the empire.

Another often overlooked feature of the war is that the rebels couldn't have won without French assistance. Looking at it from a European perspective, the American Revolution bore many similarities to the fighting, just a few years earlier, in the Seven Year's War. On that occasion Britain had allies on the continent; this time Britain had none. Since France no longer had to worry about war on the continent, it could interfere with impunity in America.

While the rebels raided British ammo dumps and arms depots, these couldn't supply an entire army, so they were able to fight on only with French-supplied weapons. This tacit support turned into naval involvement. The Royal Navy could move troops and block coastal cities at will. Because all the American colonies were relatively close to the Atlantic coast, something had to be done. Step forward the French Navy, which did an excellent job of making the journey from Britain to America even more treacherous. As the years progressed they were able to blockade the British and strangle their supply lines. All of this was vital in bringing the British to the negotiating table and forcing the Americans to create a navy from scratch (although the Americans positioned a few gun boats on the Great Lakes, they hardly constituted a navy).

In 1780 the French went further with an operation called 'Expédition Particulière', when they landed 7,000 troops, led by the Comte de Rochambeau. To put that into context, Rochambeau had more troops on the ground than George Washington. This particular expedition did very little, and Rochambeau returned to France. When he came back in 1781, he was fighting alongside Washington at the Siege of Yorktown. The British (with their German mercenaries) had been blockaded by the French Navy on one side and a Franco-American army on the other. Although the colonists did just about outnumber the French in terms of regular soldiers (rather than militia), once again the French had more men fighting than Washington had troops. This final battle in the American War of Independence would never have been decisive had it not been for the presence of the French.

29. Imperial Invention No. 3:
Industrialisation

In 1761 in Birmingham, Matthew Bolton built a steam-powered warehouse which made small metal goods. It was named the Soho Manufactory. This was the world's first factory.

The exact beginnings of the industrial revolution are much debated, but the creation of the first factory seems a good place to start. Of course, it would take generations for this one idea to catch on. Prior to the industrial revolution most labourers worked in the fields and lived in small towns. Once the industrial revolution got going, there were more people living in cities than in the countryside. Towns like Glasgow (already boosted by imperial trade) and Manchester turned into metropolises. Glasgow's population in 1780 was around 120,000; by 1811 (just a generation later), it was approaching 400,000.

No country had seen anything like it. The need for workers encouraged immigration, particularly from Ireland, which further boosted urban populations. Britain's Empire provided all the raw materials, and, in turn, these commodities were used to manufacture items that were exported around the world.

Quite why this should first happen in Britain is still a bit of a mystery. Continental Europe had its fair share of innovators; countries like France and Spain also had overseas empires with the raw materials needed to produce goods in a steam-powered factory.

You could fill a whole (dull) book on 'Why Britain?', so instead, let's consider a couple of key factors. Unlike all of its main competitors, Britain was not ruled by an autocrat. The Georges were largely ineffectual as individual rulers because it was Parliament that made the decisions. While 'democracy' was very different then from what we understand today, even in those days, it was a more flexible and efficient system than was possible under the whims of a ruler. It allowed more readily for innovation, and as the laws of the land applied to all (rather than the king being able to do what he wanted), businesses had the confidence to invest heavily in the new.

A second reason was sheer luck. Britain was blessed with coal that was both abundant and easy to access. Something had to power the steam engines – wood would do, but coal was better. The need to distribute coal (and goods) led to the construction of an elaborate system of canals and, later, railways, which revolutionised logistics and transportation.

Although this change was great for the economy and population growth overall, life for the average citizen was pretty miserable. While the lives of peasant labourers weren't great, existence in the city slums and factories was probably worse. Young children worked long hours doing dangerous jobs, for little or no pay. Wages for adults were poor, conditions were grim and industrial accidents were commonplace. Finally, the tremendous increases in urban size and density led to outbreaks of disease, the consequences of which were to be felt throughout the country – and beyond.

30. EDWARD JENNER WAS A VIRUS KILLER

By the eighteenth century smallpox was a much feared scourge. Highly infectious and regularly lethal, it often left the survivors scarred for life. The notion that exposure to a variant of the illness ('a little bit of bad') in order to build immunity had been around for millennia. However, early processes were crude, and exposure was down to blind luck.

Therefore Edward Jenner was not, technically speaking, the first person to come up with the idea of inoculation, but he was the person who made it scientific and targeted the specific pathogen of smallpox. He observed that milkmaids were generally immune to the disease and hypothesised that the pus in the blisters they received from cowpox (similar to smallpox, but much milder) protected them from smallpox.

In 1796 Jenner set out to prove his theory. He did this by inoculating eight-year-old James Phipps, the son of his gardener. Today we would regard what he did as both repugnant and immoral: Jenner scraped pus from the blisters on the hands of a milkmaid who had caught cowpox and smeared it into small incisions he had cut into the boy's arms. A few days later, James had a mild fever, indicating a minor infection. Jenner then deliberately tried to infect the boy with smallpox, and fortunately for young James, he showed complete immunity.

It was a 'Eureka' moment in medical history. Jenner had scientifically identified not only a way to combat a terrible illness, but also how to simply, and relatively safely, inoculate everyone with the world's first vaccine. Jenner submitted a paper to the Royal Society in 1797 describing his experiment but was told that his ideas were too revolutionary. He was widely ridiculed, especially by the clergy, who claimed it was ungodly to inoculate someone with diseased material. But Jenner was undaunted. He knew he was right and dedicated himself to spreading the word. With the help and support of both his colleagues and King George IV, and with financial grants from Parliament, Jenner continued to work towards his goal of inoculating entire populations. But it took until 1840 for an official Vaccination Act to really get the process going. Unfortunately Jenner didn't live to see this as he died in 1823.

However, starting from the 1840 Act, in less than 140 years the entire world had been inoculated against this illness, the only occasion in history that humans have successfully fought back against a virus and won. This is all thanks to Edward Jenner, one of the few men whose idea has saved countless lives.

Triumph came for us all in 1979 when the World Health Organization declared smallpox to be an eradicated disease ... apart from samples stored in two laboratories. Neither Russia nor America trust each other not to weaponise this terrible disease, so each keeps a protected specimen in its own sterile environment, out of the earth's biosphere ... for now.

31. MAD GEORGE WON TWO WARS BUT LOST AMERICA

George III was the first of the Georges (better known as the Hanoverians) to be born in Britain. He was the grandson of George II and the only monarch to rule during three major conflicts.

The first was the hugely successful Seven Years' War, followed by the American War of Independence – and he was still the reigning monarch during the Napoleonic era. Had Britain been an absolute monarchy, it would likely have faced disaster. These three conflicts were some of the biggest in history and certainly some of the biggest up until that point. It would have taken someone with the martial prowess of Alexander the Great or Genghis Khan to single-handedly win these sorts of wars ... and George, a quiet and reserved man, was no warrior, no Genghis Khan.

As it was the government that handled the actual planning and execution of these wars, it's the reign of George III which shows how far Parliamentary democracy had come. It was committees and councils that ran the conflicts and showed that in Britain, by the late eighteenth century, the monarch was really a figurehead. Parliamentary power gave Britain a genuine advantage as it meant it didn't need to count on the abilities of one man. This was just as well, because, while Parliament busily ran the affairs of the empire, George ... well ... George went mad.

Even though his madness is quite well known, for most of his life George didn't suffer from any unusually poor health, except for the cataracts which, in later life, steadily led to his virtual blindness.

The madness may have been caused by the blood

disease, porphyria, but is also thought to have been triggered by the death of George's favourite daughter, Princess Amelia. In 1810, aged twenty-seven, she had succumbed to complications from measles. Her early death threw George into a deep depression which seemed to bring on dementia. Add to this that, along with his eyesight, his hearing was also deteriorating, and we have a blind, deaf monarch suffering from dementia. Good job Parliament was there to take on the task of running the empire and fighting Napoleon.

The king's health deteriorated over Christmas 1819, and at one point he stayed awake for two and a half days talking virtually nonstop (it was rambling and incoherent). He finally died in January of 1820.

Although his reign had lasted nearly sixty years, it was George's last decade, known as the 'regency period', which came to define his time in power. Because his father lasted until the age of eighty-one, George junior, the fat and lazy Prince Regent, had the second longest wait to become king in British history. At the number one spot is our current Prince of Wales.

32. James Watt Reinvented the Steam Engine

We now know that the first steam engine was invented by Thomas Newcomen, whose engine was used for several generations. However, as is often the case, it's not the person who first invents something who gets the accolades, but the person who refines that something for commercial use.

In essence that's what James Watt did by producing a much improved version of the Newcomen engine in 1776 (there's that year again). Watt's version was far more efficient. Less coal was needed, making it cheaper to run, and less energy was lost, making the engine more powerful. He also was able to recreate his machine again and again, so anyone could have the exact same steam engine. While steam power had been around for most of the eighteenth century, it was James Watt who made it more efficient and turned it into the heart of industry.

It's for these reasons that it's James Watt, and not Thomas Newcomen, who gets the plaudits. It's because Watt compared the power and the use of a steam engine to that of the far more common power of a horse, that the term 'horsepower' came into usage. It was Watt's theories, combined with an outstanding mechanical legacy, that make him the father of industry. The unit of a 'watt' in terms of power is named in his honour.

33. THE FRENCH MONARCHY STARTED THE FRENCH REVOLUTION

It's not news that France was Britain's greatest rival in matters of empire, nor is it surprising that this rivalry frequently led to conflict. So it was probably only to be expected that France would back the American rebels in their war of independence. The resulting victory allowed France to revel in the defeat of its imperial competitor ... but King Louis XVI was a little uneasy about it all.

The American Revolution was not initially about being a republic; it was even mooted at one point that in the event of victory, George Washington could become the first King of America (which would have meant that America would have replaced one King George with another). However, the colony eventually chose the path to independence and turned its back on the institution of monarchy.

This meant that the French king had just backed a side that thought monarchy (in theory, any monarchy) was bad. Thousands of French soldiers, sailors and officers had fought side-by-side with men who had been subjects of the British crown and successfully overthrown it, only to return to a country that had more of an absolute monarchy than Britain. It was a recipe for revolution.

What made it worse was that during the long wars of this revolution, American celebrities, like Benjamin Franklin, were invited to the French court to extol the virtues of republicanism. And after the war, America's most important ally was France, so there was a flow of trade and ideas between the two, and many American concepts were obvious challenges to the status quo in France.

It is therefore unsurprising that when a new anti-monarch revolution erupted in Europe, it started in France. (It didn't happen in Britain, which might have been expected, since it had just lost a war with republicans in their own colonies.) Among the intelligentsia a confidence had been raised by the American Revolution that there was another way, a better way to govern ... not to mention the sheer desperation of the average French peasant, whose lot in life had barely changed since the time of knights and castles. Taxes were high and harvests were poor. They simply had nothing left to lose.

The year 1789 was the start of a period of upheaval during which Louis XVI and his family were ousted from Versailles, and feudalism was overthrown. In 1792 France was declared a republic, and Louis was beheaded, a sobering example of 'you reap what you sow'. The rest of Europe began to galvanise against this dangerous precedent of revolution and regicide (much as Europe had done against Oliver Cromwell about 150 years earlier). The revolution descended into 'the Terror', a period of mass executions and random imprisonments, when there was a complete breakdown of law and order. This intolerable situation was to lead to a period of war that would echo around the world, from 1792 to 1815 – for nearly a quarter of a century.

34. Slavery Was the Gravest Mark Against the British Empire

Let's talk about the gravest mark against the British Empire – slavery. It is a deeply unpleasant fact that slavery has been inherent in all the civilisations of the world, and it is not exclusively a white on black crime. African tribes would take enemy tribe members as their slaves. The Aztecs turned captured warriors into their slaves (or sacrifices). The Ottoman Empire needed thousands of slaves to become soldiers or concubines for the sultan. There are quotes in both the Old and New Testaments that instruct slaves to obey their masters, so even the Bible does not condemn what is now considered to be one of the most morally outrageous of crimes. Slavery was part of global civilisation for thousands of years, and no culture thought it was wrong for a very long time.

As far as British history is concerned, there were slaves in Anglo-Saxon England, and the English had been turned into slaves both by the Romans and Vikings. But it was the British Empire that turned slavery into an industrial scale enterprise.

After the restoration of the monarchy, Britain found peace and prosperity again. Newfound disposable income could be spent on luxuries such as coffee, tea, sugar and tropical fruits. These goods fetched enormous prices, particularly sugar. The tradesmen of Britain would go to the coast of Africa, where they would trade the output of Britain's workshops for slaves. They would then sail to the Caribbean, where slaves were needed to work on the sugar cane plantations. Sugar cane was such a tough crop to grow and refine that only slaves were considered to be suitable for the back-breaking work. Here the slaves were traded for sugar, which was taken back to Britain. This trading pattern was to last for at least 120 years.

This triangle made Britain's economy boom and as it grew, so did its merchant navy. To protect these investments, Britain's fighting navy also grew, and it was this process that was to make Britain the most powerful country on earth. All of this was built on the back of slaves and a desire for luxury. It's estimated that around 11 million Africans were sold into slavery, and that's not including the children who were then born into slavery. Born a slave, what chance did that child have?

The Europeans (and it wasn't just the English) who took African slaves didn't go into the interior of that continent to find tribes and round them up. Europeans generally died when they went into the African interior, largely from tropical diseases. Trading posts were created where Africans would bring captured enemies and sell them. Africa was not a nation but a continent of warring groups, just like Europe; and again, just like Europe, Africans were more than capable of carrying out horrifying acts of violence against each other. This was the dark heart of all empires.

35. An Artillery Officer Shook the World

In 1785 at the elite École Militaire in Paris, a young officer cadet was struggling. His father's death meant he had to rush through the two-year course in just twelve months. He came forty-second out of fifty-eight, but he got a commission. The cadet was a good mathematician, which meant that an artillery career beckoned, but as it was a time of peace, he toyed with the idea of going to the Ottoman Empire where he could work in the artillery corps.

This callow youth was a good gardener but terrible at dancing and foreign languages. He had a surname that clearly showed his Corsican ancestry, and he was mocked for having an unsophisticated accent. The newly graduated officer was called Napoleon Bonaparte. It is worth adding some colour to a man like this because so many people have written about his time in power that it often seems as if he was barely human.

The reality is that Napoleon was lucky, but he knew how to use his luck. Saying this in no way diminishes his astounding achievements. Plenty of people in history have been given a moment to impact events and either missed it or ended up with their head on a spike. Napoleon kept making the right choices for years.

The French wars in the late eighteenth and early nineteenth century have become known as the 'Napoleonic Wars', and because it's an easy catchall title, I will also use the term. But, in 1792, Napoleon was twenty-three and had no impact on the first few years of conflict. However, in 1795, through sheer brute force, he stabilised Paris for the National

Convention and was given command of the Army of Italy as a reward. It could be seen as a wedding present because, just a few days earlier, he had married Joséphine de Beauharnais.

It was 1796 when the world first took note of Napoleon. Rather than using his army to secure France's borders (as he had been ordered to do), he attacked Italy and, in one campaign, turned this under-equipped army into the country's conquerors. This brought stability to France and earned Napoleon immediate fame and wealth. In less than a year, this new general had achieved what so many kings and emperors had failed to do for centuries.

However, it's impossible to please everyone, and even though he had set aside a palace for his new bride, Joséphine refused to come as she was busy having an affair with a dashing cavalry lieutenant (what do you have to do to please some women?).

Napoleon, ever one to spot an opportunity, used his newfound fame and power to carry out a coup against the National Convention. 1792 marked the start of the wars, but it was 1796 that marked the start of Napoleon. He became, at first, *de facto* king and was later crowned emperor of France – as well as most of Europe.

36. William Wilberforce Conducted the First Human Rights Campaign

While Napoleon was becoming a power in Europe, the slave trade continued. Even though it was still lucrative and even though the country was fighting a war it was in danger of losing, Britain, remarkably, spent time, effort and resources to dismantle slavery.

In the late eighteenth century some Christian organisations in Britain began questioning that if 'all men are created in the image of God', what gives us the right to sell some of them like cattle? Humans weren't possessions, no matter what their skin colour. The whole system had to be morally wrong.

Some tried to defend the indefensible by making outright racist claims that the white man was superior. I will give this offensive argument no more space than it deserves.

In the late 1780s an MP called William Wilberforce decided to end this most repugnant of trades. Josiah Wedgwood (the famous potter) mass-produced a brooch with the picture of a slave and the words 'Am I not a man and a brother'. Books discussed the inhuman conditions on slave ships; some were written by ex-slaves like Olaudah Equiano, describing what slavery was like. They became must-reads in influential circles.

This was the start of the first human rights campaign and the first example of ordinary citizens wearing a symbol to advertise their cause. Events like Band Aid can trace their origins back to the tactics used to heighten the awareness among the people who mattered, to put an end to the slave trade.

The campaign would have succeeded earlier had

it not been for the wars with France. However, to Wilberforce's credit, and despite serious threats of invasion and regular news of defeats in Europe, he persevered and kept the momentum going. In 1792 the country of Sierra Leone was created by Britain as a place for ex-slaves to settle. The country was not well run (and still has serious challenges), so it was not a smooth start, but it was a start.

With war still raging, Parliament passed the Slave Trade Act in 1807. This was not a simple emancipation of slaves – it put a stop to the entire British slave trade. It also authorised naval patrols to prevent trading posts from being used for the purpose of trade in human beings, and as Britain had the world's largest commercial and military fleets, it made it difficult for everyone else to continue.

Britain was the first to do this, ahead of the Catholic Church or even African cultures. Britain led the way and would shape the world's view of slavery. It would take the rest of Europe decades to catch up, and in America, where it is said 'all men are created equal', it would take another two generations and a bloody civil war to settle the matter once and for all. Making slavery a dirty word was a British invention we can be proud of.

37. NAPOLEON INTENDED TO INVADE INDIA ... VIA EGYPT

The nearest Egypt gets to India is about 2,500 miles. They are countries on separate continents. Yet, in 1798 Napoleon invaded Egypt with the express purpose of linking up with Tipu Sultan (an Indian ruler) and together attacking the British in India. Geography to one side, it was not an insane idea. Egypt was the halfway point between Britain and India. Also, Egypt had coasts on the Mediterranean Sea and the Indian Ocean, handy staging posts.

However, Egypt had not been France's enemy, and even though the rest of Europe was still fighting France, this looked like a very odd distraction. But Napoleon didn't concern himself only with ships, supplies and soldiers; he also brought a small army of scientists. This was not only a military campaign, but also a voyage of discovery, and a number of scientific breakthroughs can be linked to this expedition.

While Napoleon was busy beating the Mamelukes and enforcing French republican power in the Muslim Middle East, he allowed the French fleet (under Vice-Admiral François-Paul Brueys d'Aigalliers) to anchor in Aboukir Bay, about twenty miles from Napoleon's base in Alexandria. Brueys had seventeen warships and believed the bay gave him a superb defensive position in case the Royal Navy turned up. So far Brueys had done an excellent job of evading the Royal Navy and getting Napoleon to his destination without a fight. Napoleon, however, had a habit of underestimating the Royal Navy and on this occasion, miscalculation led to the Battle of the Nile.

Brueys's opponent was none other than (then rear

admiral) Horatio Nelson. Nelson was not only a genius naval tactician, but he also believed in his men. He allowed his officers to deviate from his plans, provided they were carried out in spirit.

At the Battle of the Nile (which actually wasn't fought on the Nile) Brueys had anchored his ships near the coast. However, he didn't go near enough, and the slightly smaller British fleet split in two, with half of the ships slipping behind the French fleet, while the others attacked in the expected way. The French were receiving withering volleys of cannon fire from both sides.

The fighting was brutal. Nelson was wounded by shrapnel to the forehead, but Brueys was cut nearly in half by a cannon ball. He was propped up in a barrel, still issuing orders until he bled out. Shortly after that, his flagship exploded. It was such a gigantic fireball and such an instant and tremendous loss of life that all fighting stopped as both sides came to the aid of the few survivors.

The French had resisted stoutly. A couple of French ships escaped, but most were either sunk or captured. The battle stopped the French navy from being a threat in the Mediterranean and destroyed Napoleon's plans to use Egypt as a French base. It also stranded Napoleon in the Middle East. For Nelson, it was one of his most complete victories.

38. THE BRITISH MUSEUM IS FULL OF NON-BRITISH ARTEFACTS

One of the reasons Napoleon took 167 scientists as part of his Egypt invasion was due to the impact of the Enlightenment and the Scientific Revolution. Both were eighteenth-century movements to take learning, politics and society out of the superstitious past and to look at the world through a lens of logic and science.

The British Empire was at the very forefront of these movements. Charles II had founded the Royal Society to bring together the great minds of the age to share knowledge and ideas. The medieval universities were well established and well regarded when another centre of learning came along.

The British Museum was founded in 1753 with some 70,000 items given to the nation by Sir Hans Sloane, and in 1757, King George II donated the Old Royal Library. Along with his books and manuscripts, he gave the museum the right to a copy of every work published in the country, guaranteeing a world class (and constantly growing) library. It was opened to the public in 1759.

From the museum's beginnings, rich benefactors were continually adding to the collections, showing the preoccupation of the day for the ancient and exotic. While the British Museum houses the Anglo-Saxon burial goods of Sutton Hoo (discovered in 1939), it is largely full of non-British artefacts, which makes its name somewhat misleading.

Although to the modern archaeologist or anthropologist the eighteenth- and nineteenth-century collections look somewhat sensationalist, they were the triggers for a greater understanding of the world.

In the medieval era, lands that could only be imagined were portrayed with pictures of men with the heads of dogs, and faraway seas were thought to be populated with giant serpents. Now people demanded to know what was really there.

Voyages like those of Captain Cook or scientific journeys to uncover the ancient civilisations of Egypt or Babylon could count on funding, thanks to the excitement generated by the displays in the British Museum – and the other museums that were being founded in its wake.

In 1802 King George III donated the Rosetta Stone, an inscribed black stone that had been part of a wall in Egypt but had been understood to be something far more important by the French in Egypt. However, after the Battle of the Nile, the British had the upper hand, and the stone ended up in Britain. The Rosetta Stone has the same inscription in three different languages – Demotic, Greek and hieroglyphics. The fact that the inscription was a series of translations allowed the decipherment of the ancient Egyptian hieroglyphics, a language that had remained silent for more than 2,000 years.

The British Museum is a symbol of the British Empire's desire to learn as well as to rule. It continues to grow and add to our understanding of the cultures of the world. Today it has over 8 million items in its collection, and millions from around the world come to visit it every year.

39. ARTHUR WELLESLEY FIRST MADE AN IMPRESSION IN INDIA

Arthur Wellesley was born in 1769 in Dublin. When queried about his insistence on being regarded as English, despite his Irish birth, he retorted, 'And if I was born in a stable, would that make me a horse?'

His early military career was completely undistinguished, but he managed to pay his way up to the rank of major before heading to India. The British Empire, although gravely concerned about the growing power of Napoleon, still had an empire to run, and that meant dealing with other hostile neighbours; in this case, Tipu Sultan of Mysore (an area of south-west India larger than Britain).

Wellesley broke into the public consciousness at the Siege of Seringapatam in 1799. It helped that the governor-general of the East India Company was Arthur's brother Richard; but while the connection got Wellesley the job, he still had to plan the campaign and make sure he won the war. Wellesley showed he was a careful planner, which meant he lost fewer men than many to illness or desertion. It also meant morale was higher, and his troops were less tired when he needed them to go into battle.

For weeks Wellesley manoeuvred his artillery to batter the walls of the fortified palace of Seringapatam, home of Tipu Sultan. Eventually a breach was made, and it was time for an assault. In an unusual move, Wellesley chose to attack in the early afternoon, the hottest part of the day. It was hoped that even though his troops would feel the sweltering heat, the defenders would be out of position, taking refreshment.

Given covering fire by the artillery, seventy-six

British red coats led the charge of Wellesley's Anglo-Indian forces. The troops were ordered to fix bayonets, surged forwards towards the breach in the crumbling walls and scaled the ramparts.

During the ensuing fight a fat Indian officer was seen to be using hunting rifles to shoot British troops. The officer was killed, but it was only when the bodies were later examined that the Brits realised they had killed Tipu Sultan.

The so-called Fourth Anglo-Mysore War ended with the death of the ferocious Tipu Sultan and complete victory for the East India company. For Arthur Wellesley this final battle of that war led to a significant increase in his fame and personal wealth.

A few years later, Wellesley was again fighting a large Indian empire, but this time it was the Marathas. The pivotal moment was the Battle of Assaye. The battle was so heavily contested that two of the horses he rode during the battle were killed by musket fire. Wellesley personally kept his men together, and his army of fewer than 10,000 defeated an army of 50,000. He did this by keeping a cool head and attacking at the right moment, a lesson he never forgot. Shortly afterwards, Wellesley was made a member of the Most Honourable Order of the Bath. It was much later on that he became the 1st Duke of Wellington.

40. The British Empire Had Two Chief Exports

It wasn't James Cook in the eighteenth century, but the Dutch in 1606, who were the first Europeans to discover Australia, which they named 'New Holland'. However, it was the British in the late eighteenth century who started colonising. Australia became an area of interest after Britain had lost the American colonies and needed new lands for settlement.

Britain had devised a cunning plan that killed two birds with one stone. Prisons were expensive, so why not cut costs by turning an inhospitable country into a prison? It also guaranteed the settlement of a British colony in a new territory that almost nobody would have wanted to live in. In 1787 the 'First Fleet' departed from England with 1,530 people, including dozens of children, under the command of Captain Arthur Phillip. They arrived at Botany Bay but quickly moved to another area named Port Jackson (which was later renamed Sydney) on 26 January 1788, now known as Australia Day.

The arrival of the fleet marked the beginning of decades of forced immigration to the continent. Life was tough for the new 'Australians', but this was the way of things in the era of empire. For centuries Britons had either been forced or chose to go to far-off lands to start again. By the end of the empire, tens of millions had left Britain (and Ireland) to travel to the four corners of the world. Sometimes they would marry locals. In the early eighteenth century there was an expectation that 'Anglo-Indians' would become the dominant race on the sub-continent. This was a clear indication that Britain's DNA was one of its biggest exports. No other country can claim to have started colonies as far flung as Canada, New Zealand, Hong Kong and South Africa. It also means that dozens of countries around the world have had their genetic makeup permanently changed.

The other great export that spread from Britain was the English language. More than a billion people can speak it, and while it is not the most spoken language in the world (that honour belongs to Mandarin Chinese), it is the most important second language. In essence, if a company or country wants to communicate across the globe, then English is the best language to learn. It is still the primary language in the United States, South Africa, Singapore, New Zealand and Jamaica. English is regarded as essential even in countries where it is not the primary language, such as India or Sweden (which was never part of the British Empire).

This spread of the language is an echo of empire because, quite frankly, as languages go, English is not that great. It has a crazy spelling system, a subtle word order, plenty of irregular verbs and pretty much breaks all of its own rules. But for anyone born into an English speaking culture, the advantages are enormous, all thanks to the widespread influence of the British Empire.

41. KANDY IS DANGEROUS

As we saw with Arthur Wellesley in India, Britain had other battles to fight during the Napoleonic Wars. An example of a forgotten colonial war was the First Kandyan War from 1803–5 (there would be two more brief resumptions of the conflict over the next twelve/thirteen years). Kandy was the capital city of the autonomous Kingdom of Kandy in Sri Lanka.

Trade and diplomatic agreements had broken down between the Kandyan government, located in the mountainous centre of the island, and the British, who were based on the coast. To resolve matters, the British decided to invade the capital. The way was secret and well-guarded, making this perfect ambush territory, so the advantage was with the inhabitants. But it was tropical diseases that did more to harm the British forces than any hostilities.

When the imperial troops finally arrived in the capital, they found it deserted and on fire – they had captured the shell of a city. As the British pondered the situation, the Kandy slowly took over all the outposts around the palace complex and attacked the main garrison. The fighting was desperate, but the British clung on. In the end the Kandy agreed to honour the negotiated terms of withdrawal, but of the 149 Europeans too sick to be moved, all but two were butchered. One man was stripped, beaten unconscious and hung by the neck; however, the rope broke and when he awoke he found himself in a pile of bodies and was able to escape to tell of the horrific slaughter.

This nasty and forgotten war is singled out for two reasons. Firstly, it's a reminder that even though the British were the invaders, not all of the atrocities were perpetrated by those wearing red jackets. Military records of the eighteenth and nineteenth centuries reveal numerous occasions when British troops were captured and then executed or tortured, or, in some cases, eaten. It is a modern myth that local cultures were always more peaceful or more worthy than those of imperial Britain. War, it seems, brings out the worst in all cultures.

Secondly, it's important because at the time this was seen as a minor colonial campaign even though thousands died on both sides. Today, after twelve years' of fighting, 500 British casualties in Afghanistan are considered a heavy price to pay, so it's worth pointing out that these short, sharp imperial engagements were actually far more costly in terms of British lives.

With all the resources of an empire and a healthy technological advantage, the British were able to grind down the Kingdom of Kandy, and while uprisings rumbled on, the main fighting was over by 1805.

The First Kandyan War is by no means the only forgotten war of this era. Another will be explored later, but a few more of the forgotten wars include the Gurkha War, the First Burma War and the Ashanti War of the Golden Stool, to name a few of the more exotic ones.

42. NELSON ATTACKED A CITY WITH SHIPS

In 1801 Nelson was fighting an epic sea battle once again; however, almost everything about it was unusual.

Since Britain was not at war with Denmark, it was odd to find the Royal Navy attacking Danish ships in the harbour at Copenhagen. Not unusually, the situation was complicated; alliances often blurred. Essentially the British feared a potential alliance between Russia and the Scandinavians, which would then threaten Britain from the north, rather than just the usual threats from the French and Spanish to the south. The attacks were meant to warn the Danes to keep away from trouble, and while a battle wasn't actively sought, that's what Nelson got.

Nelson's commander, Admiral Sir Hyde Parker, made it clear that he didn't want to go on this mission. Regarded as a fairly irresolute officer, his lack of resolve was compounded by the fact that the sixty-one-year-old Parker had just married eighteen-year-old Frances Onslow, so he was quite keen to see action of another kind.

A third oddity arose from the assumption that when a fleet is safely anchored in its capital, with cover from heavy shore batteries, it is usually thought to be safe. Nelson attacked with full force, knowing he would come under fire, not just from the cannons on the ships, but from the other larger pieces on shore. It was during this pivotal action that Nelson assumed Parker (who had the bigger and heavier ships that could soak up more damage) would join him. Instead, Parker raised the flags for Nelson to disengage. Nelson chose not to, remarking, 'I only have one eye, I have the right to be blind sometimes.'

In the heat of battle Nelson was seen writing a letter to the Danes. The damage and loss of life on Nelson's ships was heavy, so an officer enquired as to why, under the circumstances, he would spend time on a letter. Nelson replied that he wanted to give the illusion that he could afford to write a letter of such length. It worked. As the Danes had suffered even heavier casualties than the Brits, a ceasefire was readily agreed.

Negotiations began the next day, and Britain got what it wanted – Denmark agreed to stay out of the war. This battle may have been won by a certain amount of subterfuge on Nelson's part, but, in essence, this was an ugly slugging match. As this was an epic artillery duel, little skill other than holding your nerve was needed. This was Nelson's hardest-won battle, and he was made a viscount for his bravery. Admiral Parker got his own reward as he was able to return, in one piece, to his blushing bride.

43. Wellington Spent a Lot of Time in Spain and Portugal

One of the reasons why the Napoleonic Wars are better remembered than others is because of a satisfying narrative. Napoleon was the victor most of the time, but a rising British star arrives, and in a final showdown Napoleon comes undone. Ultimately, the Napoleonic Wars become the story of the two greatest military leaders of their day.

However, Arthur Wellesley's arrival in the Napoleonic Wars began in a rather underwhelming manor. Dispatched to Portugal to fight Napoleon's army, he quickly realised he was outnumbered and likely to be outmanoeuvred, so he went quiet – for months. His army was apparently inactive. He did not advance, and his reports back to Britain were bland and perfunctory. Public opinion turned against him. It was only his family connections in the cabinet that prevented him from being recalled in disgrace. But, when the French finally attacked, Wellesley sprung his daring trap.

For months he had been busy building a line of defences at Torres Vedras. When the French attacked, Wellesley had 152 forts and 628 redoubts ready. As he and his army retreated to these fortifications, they destroyed any food or resources the French could use. By not informing his high command, Wellesley had ensured complete surprise. When the French arrived at the defences their general declared, 'The devil cannot surely have built these mountains.'

The French assault was easily repelled and led to a standoff, during which the French army slowly wasted away due to lack of food. If the French invasion had been an incoming tide, it broke on the walls of Torres Vedras and after that, ebbed away, allowing Wellesley to push into Spain.

It's not generally realised just how much time Wellesley spent fighting in Spain and Portugal, and because he sometimes fought with the brave and often brutal Spanish irregular forces, these are the ones who get the plaudits in modern day Spain. Wellesley is a passing figure in the history of their war with France. (While this might seem unfair, the British later do the same with Waterloo; it was not just the British who fought Napoleon). During his time in these two countries, Wellesley fought every kind of skirmish, ambush, siege and pitched battles. The epic battle at Salamanca did much to bring freedom to Spain and liberated Madrid. At the time Wellesley was lavishly rewarded, not just by the Brits, but by the Portuguese and Spanish too.

So in 1813 when everywhere things were going badly wrong for Napoleon, Wellesley was already in northern Spain. From there was able to move into France, his army the first to do so, beating the Prussians, Austrians and Russians. Up until this point, Wellesley had defeated Napoleon only by proxy. The two giants had yet to face off in a final battle that neither could afford to lose. It's this story arc that fits so well into a film or book.

44. A Self-Taught Clockmaker Solved the Problem of Longitude

The Royal Navy is synonymous with the British Empire. Putting it simply, without the navy, there wouldn't have been an empire. However, traversing the world's oceans is considerably easier said than done. Finding your way around a land mass is relatively easy as there will be landmarks or someone to ask the way. Not so on the thousands of miles of featureless ocean.

To know where you are on a ship, you have to work out your latitude and longitude. Latitude can be measured using the sun as a guide, but longitude (how far east or west you are) is much harder.

In the end it was a self-taught clockmaker, by the name of John Harrison, who invented a wind-up clock that lost very little time, even on a moving ship. His so-called 'marine chronometer' established an official solution to what was thought to be an intractable problem. It earned Harrison the Longitude Prize (and a substantial amount of money) in 1773. With his chronometer, sailors were able to calculate a ship's longitude and, therefore, to gauge its position. However, the first chronometers were very expensive, and most ships could not afford one; therefore, for at least a generation or so after this, there were still difficulties working out time and, consequently, longitude.

The need to agree the zero point of longitude took far longer. It wasn't until 1884 that Greenwich, England, was internationally agreed to be the fixed zero point.

45. BRITAIN'S GREATEST NAVAL VICTORY LED TO MASS MOURNING

Rarely does one battle bring dominance to one side's forces for over a century, and rarely does a war hero die in the middle of his greatest victory. Both of these can be said of Nelson at Trafalgar.

In 1805 the French fleet was, once again, proving to be a threat to the British Isles, and this time they were supported by the Spanish fleet. In general, French and Spanish warships were bigger than British ones, which meant more cannons, more men to fire them and more men to board in the event of close-quarter fighting. So in October, when Nelson's thirty-three ships met an armada of forty-one enemy vessels, things weren't looking good.

Nelson wanted to repeat the tactics of the Battle of the Nile and had his fleet divide into two parallel lines to sail perpendicular to the enemy ships. This would split the Franco-Spanish fleet into sections, with the front section having to turn around (a challenging manoeuvre that depends on wind direction) so that the advantage of numbers would be lost. It also meant the British fleet would be under enemy cannon fire as it advanced and would be unable to return fire. It was a bold and risky plan, but if it worked it would win the battle.

Nelson started by ordering the raising of flags that said, 'ENGLAND EXPECTS THAT EVERY MAN WILL DO HIS DUTY' (at the time, the term 'England' and 'Britain' were interchangeable, so no snub was directed at the other nations of Great Britain).

The Battle of Trafalgar happened just off the Spanish shore, on such a beautiful autumn day that onlookers came to see it. The wind was light, meaning the ships appeared to move and change direction as if in slow motion.

Once the ships came crashing into each other, Nelson insured the *Victory* (his ship) was in the very heart of the battle. When *Victory* exchanged fire with the French ship *Redoubtable*, it became obvious that its rigging had been turned into a snipers' nest. One of the marksmen took aim at a group of officers (it was tough to hit a single man in the rolling seas with all the smoke and noise of battle – better to aim at a group) and fired.

The sharpshooter's bullet entered Nelson's left shoulder and travelled down his body, rupturing an artery and shattering several vertebrae. They were fatal wounds. Nelson lived long enough to know victory had been secured. Almost as soon as the battle ended, a three-day storm further damaged the enemy's remaining ships. It was as if the sea itself mourned Nelson's passing.

Back home, the news of Nelson's death caused a national outpouring of grief. Britain's most famous and most daring naval officer was dead. Who would save them now?

They needn't have worried. Britain's consistent victories, combined with the world's largest fleet, meant the Royal Navy experienced no serious challenges until the First World War, more than a century later.

46. Imperial Invention No. 4: The Steam Train

A steam engine isn't the same thing as a steam locomotive. But by the late eighteenth century, small models of machines that could move by steam power were being built in various parts of Britain. However, it was Richard Trevithick, a mining engineer, who built the first full-scale working railway steam locomotive. The unnamed engine went on its maiden journey in Wales in February of 1804.

After this it didn't take long for all kinds of steam locomotives to be built, with railways big and small seeming to sprout out of the ground. But the problem with these very early models (like Trevithick's) was that they simply weren't very fast or energy efficient. It takes a lot of energy to produce speeds that a horse could still beat.

George Stephenson, another engineer, worked on these early designs in order to improve them. Perhaps the most famous of the early steam trains was Stephenson's *Rocket*, a locomotive that could travel up to twenty-eight miles per hour, a speed unheard of at the time. To the modern eye, his design looks most like what we think of as a 'train'. It was the first of the many steam-powered vehicles to be of practical use and became the blueprint for future steam locomotives.

The railways revolutionised British society. Now goods, people and news travelled faster than ever, giving Britain yet further advantages over other competitor countries.

47. A Small Town in Belgium Became Very Famous

By the start of 1815 Europe was at peace once again. Napoleon had been defeated and exiled to Elba; the rest of Europe settled down to business as usual, and France had a new king, Louis XVIII (so that made the previous twenty-six years of war and revolution worth it).

However, in March Napoleon escaped his island banishment, arrived in France and quickly rallied his veteran troops for one last stab at dominance. Europe's armies had largely demobilised, and this was yet another example of Napoleon's bold moves, giving him the momentum and advantage, even though the whole of Europe was against him.

Only one man and one army were close enough to nip this resurrection in the bud and that was Arthur Wellesley, now the 1st Duke of Wellington, with the British army ... and the Prussians ... and the Dutch ... and the German forces of Hanover, Nassau and Brunswick. However, in Britain today, we remember this as a solely a British affair, with a little help from the Prussians.

There can be no doubt, however, that Wellington was in charge, and it was the British forces that were the key to resistance. On 16 June the Prussians were defeated at Ligny, and at Quatre Bras, the fierce Dutch resistance was nearly overwhelmed by the sheer weight of French numbers – until Wellington arrived with British reinforcements. This meant that rather than continuing his advance, Napoleon now faced a man he had fought by proxy on a number of occasions. The site of this confrontation was the small town of Waterloo.

The two armies met on 18 June. Wellington had positioned most of his forces just behind the crest of some high ground where the French artillery could do little damage. Napoleon was not himself on the day as his haemorrhoids were so painful he couldn't ride his horse, so he couldn't use his own tactical brilliance to exploit any weaknesses in the Anglo-Dutch defences. At one point he even left the battle to rest.

The centre turned into a slugging match as both sides added reinforcements and blasted away at each other. (Note: the charge of the British heavy cavalry at Waterloo suffered greater casualties than the infamous Charge of the Light Brigade a generation later in the Crimean War.)

Wellington was able to hold back the French until the Prussians arrived, just as Napoleon had simply run out of men, options and energy. It was a crushing defeat. Napoleon fled into the night, only to be caught and exiled to the remote island of St Helena, where he died in 1821.

As Wellington surveyed the huge amount of death and destruction on a battlefield where more than 50,000 men lay dead or wounded after just one day's fighting, he observed that it had been a close-run thing. He also said (far more poignantly), 'Believe me, nothing except a battle lost can be half so melancholy as a battle won.'

48. THERE IS NOTHING LIKE AN ENGLISH ECCENTRIC

You know those stories of British aristocrats behaving outrageously? Well, John 'Mad Jack' Mytton is the very epitome of these. Mental healthcare, such as it was in the nineteenth century, depended on wealth. Poor people were ignored, forced to beg or sometimes locked up in horrific places like Bedlam. Locals would pay to see the disturbed individuals who were often kept in cages. It was barbaric. However, bizarre behaviour in the wealthy was classified as 'eccentric', which made everything okay. John Mytton clearly needed help, but he was simply too headstrong (and too wealthy) to be stopped. Everything you are about to read is absolutely true.

Mytton's behaviour, even as a child, was problematic. Always in trouble, he once got into a fight with a teacher at Westminster School, which resulted in his being home schooled. His private tutors also dealt with strange behaviour (like leaving a horse in the tutor's bedroom). Later on he joined the army, just after the Napoleonic Wars, but saw no action.

In 1819 he secured his seat in Parliament by 'encouraging' the constituents of Shrewsbury to vote for him by offering them £10 notes. Unfortunately (or perhaps fortunately) he found politics boring and attended Parliament once, for thirty minutes.

With money and time on his hands, he rode his horse into the Bedford Hotel, in Leamington Spa, up the grand staircase and onto the balcony from which he jumped, still seated on his horse, over the diners in the restaurant below, out through the window and onto the Parade. All of this for a bet.

Jack kept numerous pets, including some 2,000 dogs, at his ancestral home of Halston Hall. His favourites were fed on steak and champagne. Some dogs wore livery and others were costumed. A favourite horse had free range inside the manor and would lie in front of the fire with his owner.

Jack loved hunting and preferred to do so naked. He was even seen naked in the snow, gun in hand. He also loved a dare and would drive his gig at high speed at an obstacle like a rabbit hole, simply to discover if the carriage would turn over. Another time he wanted to see if a horse pulling a carriage could jump over a tollgate. It could not. Jack managed to survive these incidents without serious injuries.

Apparently without any regard for his own welfare, Jack picked a fight with a tough Shropshire miner who had disturbed his hunt. The bare knuckle fight lasted twenty rounds before the miner gave up. In yet another incident, he tried to rid himself of hiccups by setting fire to his nightshirt. He suffered no serious injury, and to be fair, it did get rid of the hiccups.

Any number of medical diagnoses might come to mind today, but a lot of Jack's wild behaviours might have had to do with the fact that he could drink eight bottles of port a day.

49. Peterloo Was a Very English Atrocity

After winning a war, building an empire and starting the industrial revolution, it could be assumed that, by 1819, the British economy was doing well. But it wasn't. Poor crops, high taxes and low wages were leading to a crisis on a national scale.

The common man didn't have much of a voice in the rapidly industrialising Midlands and northern England. The continuation of the traditional political system meant that the rapidly growing populations of cities like Manchester had the same representation after industrialisation as they had before. The people felt disenfranchised and as if they had nothing to lose. This was an explosive combination.

A peaceful crowd gathered in St Peter's Field on 16 August to listen to political speeches. The crowd was enormous (60–80,000, almost 10 per cent of Lancashire's population). Accompanied by several hundred special constables, magistrates came to see what was going on and to determine whether the gathering or the speeches broke any laws. It's worth noting that the French Revolution and the ensuing anarchy in that country were still fresh in the public mind. While the people wanted justice, the authorities needed to keep control.

The key speaker of the day was Henry Hunt. He was a British radical who advocated parliamentary reform and the repeal of the despised Corn Laws (basically, these kept grain prices high, which adversely affected the purchasing power of the working man). As he spoke for his beliefs, William Hulton, the chairman of the magistrates, issued an arrest warrant for Hunt and the other speakers. This order and another similar one were sent to the nearby Salford Yeomanry Cavalry.

The authorities rode out to arrest the speakers and, in doing so, knocked over a woman who dropped her child, killing the two-year-old as a result of their haste. When the cavalrymen arrived at the scene, they pushed straight into the crowd, which retaliated by hurling bricks and stones. In this pivotal moment, the soldiers lost their heads and began hacking with their sabres at anyone nearby. More cavalry arrived and attempted to charge and disperse the crowd before it was realised that people were having difficulty finding exits from the field. By now the Yeomanry had completely lost any semblance of restraint.

When the dust had settled, around a dozen people were dead and 400–700 injured. It was the *Manchester Observer* that first used the term 'Peterloo', thereby combining the name of the field and the famous battle to conjure up an image of carnage on home soil. The immediate response by the government was not one of compassion. Instead, it cracked down on any proposals for reform and tried to crush the radical movement. Hunt and eight others were tried in 1820, charged with sedition and found guilty.

This is one of the most shameful events in British imperial history on the home front.

50. Britain Had Many Rotten Boroughs

In the nineteenth century Britain was technically a democracy, but Peterloo showed there was still a long way to go. Britain had many 'rotten boroughs', areas with electorates dominated by an aristocratic family, who had most or all of the votes. For example, in the 1831 general election, 88 of the 406 Members of Parliament were voted in by fewer than fifty voters. Without question, something needed to be done.

The Reform Act of 1832 redistributed the electoral areas to do away with the rotten boroughs and gave the massive urban populations of the industrial heartlands more of a say. After this, about one in six adult males had the right to vote. There was still no universal suffrage, but it was a start.

Further reforms dragged on as the Whigs, Liberals and Conservatives argued about exactly what a modern democracy should look like. It wasn't until 1867 that the Second Reform Act was finally passed. This was essentially an act of universal suffrage (for men), which allowed any adult male to vote. The Act had been pushed through by the Conservatives as it was thought it would help their chances in the 1868 general election, but they lost.

There was yet more delay until, a few years later, the Ballot Act of 1872 introduced something that we all take for granted in a modern democracy: the secret ballot. The Act made illegal the practice of paying or entertaining voters. Even though this meant that it was much harder for unscrupulous candidates to operate, secrecy had been opposed by the establishment, which genuinely believed that 'elders and betters' had a legitimate right to influence their tenants and underlings. Suffrage was definitely on a roll.

Ironically, the Ballot Act created the new phenomenon of campaigning as an unintended consequence. If you couldn't pay the voters, you needed to get out and spread your message with meetings and adverts in newspapers. It was a costly business and, rather counter-intuitively, led to a decline of middle-class candidates, who were unable to fund such expenses. This, in turn, led to an increase in the numbers of landed gentry who were able to gain seats in the House of Commons because only they could afford the costs involved.

Women, however, remained disenfranchised from the electoral process. At the time it was thought that women only wanted to stay at home and raise their children. It was argued that women couldn't handle the male-dominated world of politics or even that they weren't smart enough because their brains were smaller than men's. It was all deeply sexist, and it would take many decades of campaigning and a savage world war to finally achieve truly universal suffrage.

51. Princess Victoria Was Not Meant to Be Queen

George III ruled for nearly sixty years from 1760 to 1820. He was succeeded by his son, George IV, who, owing to his father's poor health, had been made prince regent. He spent years gambling, eating and drinking to excess – all while watching his father go mad.

George IV very publicly tried to divorce his wife and indulged a string of mistresses, but he was so busy with his vices that he forgot to have any legitimate children, so it was his younger brother who came to the throne in 1830 as William IV.

William had served in the Royal Navy and had never expected to be king. By the time he ascended to the throne, he was sixty-four. His only legitimate child was a daughter who died when she was two. He had ten illegitimate children, but they could not become monarch, so William looked to his favourite niece as a suitable heir. She was only eleven when he came to power, which meant that if he died before she came of age at eighteen, her mother would become regent. This was a real issue for William as he despised the Duchess of Kent, seen as cold, officious and a woman who unnecessarily smothered her daughter in unnecessary layers of protection and protocol.

At William's last birthday banquet in August of 1836, with his niece and the duchess present, he said to the gathering,

> I trust to God that my life may be spared for nine months longer ... I should then have the satisfaction of leaving the exercise of the Royal authority to the personal authority of that young lady, heiress presumptive to

the Crown, and not in the hands of a person now near me, who is surrounded by evil advisers and is herself incompetent to act with propriety in the situation in which she would be placed.

It was about as damning a statement as could be made, and, unsurprisingly, the duchess left immediately after his speech. The pressure was now on the young Princess Victoria. When she was born, she had been fifth in the line of succession after her father and his three older brothers, so the chances of her ever becoming queen were remote. However, due to deaths and the lack of legitimate children, the options dwindled, and by the time of William's speech, she was the only remaining legitimate member of the House of Hanover.

William was running a race against time in a contest between his failing health and his will to survive. But William was a stubborn old seadog and hung on until June 1837, just a month after Victoria's eighteenth birthday. It must have pleased William no end to know that he had thwarted the duchess and succeeded in achieving his greatest wish.

Unlikely ever to have ascended to the throne, it was the young Queen Victoria who would go on to rule an era so great in British history that it bears her name.

52. THE OPIUM WARS WERE THE DIRTIEST WARS IN HISTORY

By the nineteenth century, China had fallen badly behind the West in terms of learning and technology. The Confucian system may have created one of the world's most efficient bureaucracies, but it also stifled change. Blissfully unaware, China assumed it was still the centre of the universe (literally, as well as figuratively) and superior to all. It was arrogant and frustrating to deal with. The phrase to 'kow tow' comes from the Chinese demand for a kind of ritual grovelling that western diplomats had to perform before the emperor and his advisors. Britain and other western nations wanted to trade, but China didn't want to play ball.

So, in the 1830s, in an attempt to create a market, the East India Company began to export opium to the country. At the time, opium was not illegal in Britain, but its addictive nature was well known. The ploy was exploitative, cynical and amoral, designed purely to generate more 'customers', i.e. drug addicts.

The Chinese authorities protested and were lured into a diplomatic trap. When they destroyed some of the opium, they broke existing trade agreements. This illegal destruction of British property allowed the East India Company to respond with force. The result was catastrophic for China. With out-of-date weaponry, both on land and on sea, the tiny British force, supported by the Royal Navy, was unstoppable.

Opium may have been the ostensible cause of the war, but the real reason was China's refusal to trade, exacerbated by its continued arrogance in refusing to recognise anyone else as an equal (it wasn't just

Europeans who could be racist). The Chinese view was wrong, but importing hundreds of tons of narcotics into a country for the sole purpose of creating drug addicts was worse. Parliament came to its senses and stopped the war – and this is the remarkable thing about the Opium Wars: how many times has a country stopped a war it's comfortably winning because it was morally wrong to continue?

This is worth pausing to consider. Certainly it's desirable to stop a war that you are losing or to end a war that's uneconomical, but who stops a war that you are easily winning? Along with other western powers, Britain could have carved up China as it did later with Africa. But in this instance, Parliament recognised that even by the shaky standards of international law and diplomacy in the age of empires, this was not playing fair, and while the cessation of hostilities led to concessions by the Chinese, the authorities there were not nearly as punitive as they could have been. It was as a result of Chinese concessions that Britain was loaned the island that would become Hong Kong. As far as the Chinese were concerned, this began their 'century of humiliation' as western (and later, Japanese) imperial powers marched through China, almost at will.

53. WITHOUT ELECTRICITY YOU WOULD NEED A BAG OF COAL TO RUN YOUR iPAD

Danish physicist and chemist Hans Christian Ørsted realised in 1820 that an electric current could affect a magnetic field. What he didn't realise (and what wasn't officially recognised until the 1870s) was that he had shown that electricity and magnetism are actually the same force, now known as electromagnetism.

However, a year later, the young British scientist Michael Faraday went further. He positioned an electric wire through the middle of a metal ring placed in mercury and ran an electric current through the ring. The wire rotated around the inside of the ring when the current was switched on and stopped when the current was disconnected. This was what he called a homopolar motor and what we know today as an electric motor. It could, technically speaking, be considered as the next imperial invention, but, in the context of this fact, I am concerned with the man, rather than this one device.

At the time, the electric motor was regarded as a something of a novelty, but its invention was vital if the era of electronics was ever to take off. Could a computer be powered by steam? Yes, in theory, but would you be willing to carry around a bag of coal to charge up your iPad?

So while Faraday was not the brainchild behind the computer (although that man was also British), the modern world, as we know it, would not exist today had it not been for Faraday's revolutionary idea.

Later, in 1836, he developed what became known as the Faraday cage. This is an enclosure (now often seen in the form of a human-shaped cage) fabricated from a mesh of conducting material (usually steel). The cage blocks external electric fields by channelling electricity through the mesh. Essentially it shields the person inside the cage from any amount of voltage. This discovery is the basis for spectacular science experiments and magic shows. It also explains why, in the event of being caught in a lightning storm, you should stay in your car – if the car is struck by a lightning bolt, it will act as a Faraday cage.

Faraday was also the chemist who invented the Bunsen burner, discovered benzene and created processes to liquefy gases such as chlorine.

None of this would have happened had it not been for the many British scientific institutions that admitted people of all classes, as long as they were sponsored. Faraday's family was poor. His father was a blacksmith, and Faraday's first job was as a book binder. However, his access to books led to his love of learning and enabled him to attend the lectures of the esteemed scientist of his day, Humphrey Davy. Faraday took a risk and sent Davy his voluminous notes, taken during Davy's lectures. This led to a job at the Royal Institution in 1813. It was from this point onwards that the facilities of the Royal Institute allowed him to carry out his ground-breaking experiments.

54. A WAR WAS FOUGHT OVER A FLAGSTAFF

Radio carbon dating and DNA testing suggest that New Zealand was one of the last major landmasses to be settled by human beings, who seemed to have come to the islands in the mid- to late thirteenth century. Then, for centuries, they lived an isolated life. In 1642, when Dutch sailors reached the islands, their first encounters with the local Māori did not go well. In fact, four of the Dutch crew died.

New Zealand is so remote that it wasn't until 1769, with the arrival of Captain Cook, that the next Europeans made it there. At the start of the nineteenth century, when settlers began to land in numbers, the result was almost constant warfare with the Māori. The natives were a warrior people who used the dense vegetation to lay the perfect ambushes. Despite having their own traditional weapons, they also rapidly adopted gunpowder technology.

While there was a constant series of attacks, what triggered an actual war was a flagpole. In 1844 the British colonists were proudly flying the Union flag on what is now called Flagstaff Hill (for obvious reasons). A local Māori chief, frustrated by the colonists, cut down the flag. The British sent a detachment of troops to prevent trouble before it began. There were talks, and a peaceful arrangement was agreed. However, in January 1845, the flag was chopped down again. So a third (iron-encased) flag pole was erected and a guard hut placed nearby. But come the following morning, this flag pole also had been destroyed.

By now, the destruction of the flagstaff, a symbol of Māori resistance, had become a matter of principle – for both sides. In March of 1845, the fourth and final attack on the flag was a much bloodier affair. Hundreds of heavily armed Māori warriors attacked the Royal Marine garrison posted near the flagstaff. All the marines were killed, and the flag was, once again, left in the dirt. This time it was war.

The war lasted a year but ground to a stalemate when British troops were unable to gain the upper hand against the Māoris, whose bases were complex strong points with trench systems, bunkers and firing steps, intended to turn raids into sieges. Although they brought the British forces to a halt, the Māori still faced an empire with limitless resources. The subsequent fighting was bloody, and even though this was a war that Britain didn't lose, it shows that even empires with technical superiority have their limitations.

The Flagstaff War is a great example to challenge a cliché about imperial wars. The nineteenth century was not an era of automatic victory for the white man. Sometimes local tribes were outclassed and outgunned, and sometimes they simply weren't as tactically astute as their British counterparts. New Zealand would eventually become part of the British Empire but not through violence. Rather, Māori numbers diminished through disease, while British immigrants outnumbered and out-bred the local indigenous people.

55. THE BRITISH EMPIRE WAS NOT A GOOD NEIGHBOUR

England's very first overseas territory was Ireland. For 700 years or so the Emerald Isle was ruled from Britain. It is, therefore, nothing less than scandalous that the country most abused, the country which gained the least from an imperial overlord was Britain's oldest and closest possession.

That's not to say that the Irish took things lying down. There was such unrelenting discontent that British soldiers would often refer to a post in Ireland as 'going to the Irish wars'. However, the darkest chapter in Irish history was not started by the British, but by a single-celled organism called *Phytophthora infestans*, more commonly known as potato blight.

It started in 1845 when farmers began noticing black marks on the leaves of their potatoes. Digging up a potato revealed it to be tainted and inedible. Virtually the entire potato crop of that year failed. That was bad enough, but then it happened the next year and the next, all the way to 1852. A third of Irish peasants were reliant on potatoes, so this was a catastrophe on a national scale. (Note: you can survive on milk and potatoes without suffering any serious nutrient deficiencies. It's the cheapest and most basic nourishing diet, which is why it was so important in poor farming communities.)

Although the potato crop failed, Ireland was still producing and exporting more than enough grain crops to feed the population. So while the disaster was natural, it was made far worse by the gross mismanagement and indifference of the British ruling classes, who only worried about profits, rather than the hundreds of thousands of people starving to death. As the stories of desperation spread across the globe, the Ottoman Empire and even Native Americans sent food aid. The land owners, who could most immediately alleviate the situation, chose to evict the starving and impoverished from the very land that had been their homes, usually for generations.

The famine was a watershed in Irish history. Home rule had been a rallying call for a long time, but this annihilation of the population was seen as the final straw, further fanning the flames of Irish republicanism.

For those who left the country and escaped the worst, it was these memories that were etched into their minds. It was the stories of uncaring British aristocrats, passed down the generations for over a century that kept alive the antipathy and distrust towards the British government, long after the famine was over. This explains the ongoing mistrust by Irish communities in such far-flung places as Boston.

During the famine era approximately 1 million people died, and a million more emigrated from Ireland, many to America. As a result, Ireland's population fell by nearly a quarter. In the history of the British Empire, the story of Ireland is one of shame and disgrace.

56. A Geologist Caused a Religious Dilemma

For more than a millennium and a half, the age of the world had not been in any doubt. The Bible traces a family tree from Jesus back to Adam (actually there are two trees, and they contradict each other – but let's not go there). So by carefully working out the age of each of these men, you can come to a conclusion about when God created the earth. However, as scientific endeavours branched out into all areas of learning, scientific observation began bumping into cherished sacred cows.

The Scot James Hutton has often been called the 'Father of Modern Geology'. This is because he originated the theory of uniformitarianism, a fundamental principle of geology, which explains the features of the earth's crust by means of natural processes over long periods of geologic time. Through observations of phenomena such as granite schists (I'm trying not to bore you), he came to the conclusion that these rock formations occurred over extensive periods of time, and this cooling and reforming of various minerals led to the different types of rock we identify today. He took his time with this idea, and his book on the theory was published twenty-five years after it was first proposed. Attention grippingly entitled *The Theory of the Earth; or an Investigation of the Laws observable in the Composition, Dissolution, and Restoration of Land upon the Globe*, it was read (in two parts) at meetings of the Royal Society of Edinburgh.

Hutton introduced the concept that the earth evolved and changed over time, which was in contradiction to the idea that God created a perfect and unchanging world in one day.

Later, in 1862, the physicist William Thomson published *Age of the Earth: Geology and Theology*, which contained calculations that fixed the age of the earth at between 20 million and 400 million years. Thomson was a Christian and saw nothing contradictory in showing that our planet was clearly older than a family tree of unknown origin. In other words, a literal reading of the Bible was not necessary to be a good Christian.

Although Hutton's work caused religious dilemmas for some Christians, it explained why the earth's crust is the way it is. Mining goes all the way back to prehistory, but it wasn't until the nineteenth century that it became scientific. Because the locations of metal and mineral deposits could now be calculated, his findings were vital to the mining industry. While Hutton didn't go on to make further great leaps in the field of geology, he turned the study of rocks and minerals into a science, which allowed others to start assessing, annotating and comparing – and, therefore, greatly enhancing humanity's abilities to harvest precious minerals and metals from the rocks.

57. Prince Albert Made an Exhibition of Himself

The French Industrial Exposition of 1844 (the title tells you everything) was held in Paris. It was a huge success, and Britain took note. In particular, Prince Albert took note. By this time Queen Victoria had married her cousin (now known as the prince consort), who had even less power than the queen, all but a figurehead herself. The French exposition inspired Prince Albert to hold a similar event to showcase Britain's industrial progress.

So The Great Exhibition of the Works of Industry of all Nations was born. It later became known simply as 'The Great Exhibition'. Helped by prestigious members of the Royal Society, Albert designed the exhibition for 'the encouragement of Arts, Manufactures and Commerce as a celebration of modern industrial technology and design'.

The Crystal Palace was specifically built to house this showcase of achievement. A massive cast-iron greenhouse, its structure contained 84,000 m² of glass and stood until 1936 when it burned down (it was very unlucky for a structure made almost entirely of iron and glass to burn down). The palace contained 92,000 m² of floor space and accommodated a colossal 14,000 exhibitors.

The exhibition was an enormous success, with more than 6 million visitors. It turned a profit too, making £186,000, which was used to found the Victoria and Albert Museum, the Science Museum and the Natural History Museum.

For a man without much in the way of real power, Prince Albert created a stunning legacy.

58. HALF A MILLION PEOPLE DIED OVER A CHURCH ORNAMENT

The Church of the Nativity in Bethlehem is a long way from Paris, Moscow and London, and yet it was the placement of a silver star Christmas ornament in that church that was to lead to war between three major European powers.

The holy Christian sites had been under Muslim rule since the time of the Crusades, and by the nineteenth century they had been overseen by the Ottoman Empire for centuries. However, in 1852, Emperor Napoleon III sent a silver star to the Church of the Nativity and declared France as the protector of Catholics in the Middle East. The Ottomans allowed its placement, but Russia objected on the grounds that it was the protector of Orthodox Christians, and the star implied a Catholic supremacy. The Ottoman authorities tried to appease them by removing the star, but that, of course, insulted the French. When the star 'disappeared', it was enough for Russia to send forces into the Danube area.

The silver star incident was the pretext Russia wanted to flex its muscles after a century of imperial gains. But France and Britain were not prepared to tolerate further Russian expansion and backed the weakened Ottoman Empire to stop it from possible collapse in the face of Russian ambitions.

Fighting took place in the Baltic, the Caucuses and the Crimea. At the time it was referred to as the Russian War but became known as the Crimean War. This was the largest conflict Victorian troops would have to fight and is probably best known for the botched charge of the Light Brigade at the Battle of Balaclava.

The war had some interesting unintended consequences. It was the first war to have a war correspondent in Sir William Howard Russell, who sent articles to *The Times*. For the first time ever, the population in a country at war could read regular reports about what was going on. The descriptions of common soldiers fighting so valiantly led to the first medal that a non-commissioned officer could win: the Victoria Cross (every one of these medals has been made from cannons captured in this war).

It was the first war to be photographed. As poor hygiene was an issue, soldiers were told not to shave, and their big, bushy beards in photos would become associated with manliness and the military, so opulent facial hair became the fashion.

This was the first major war to use steam trains to get supplies to the front line. The cold weather led to the invention of the balaclava and the cardigan (after Lord Cardigan). Florence Nightingale and Mary Seacole helped to improve hospital sanitation. Finally, up until this war, tobacco was smoked in pipes, but Turkish troops were wrapping their tobacco in cartridge papers, the forerunner of the cigarette.

Two and a half years and half a million dead later, Russia signed a peace treaty. Most importantly, the silver star was returned to the Church of the Nativity.

59. A Lie Started a War

The Indian Mutiny is sometimes called the Indian Rebellion of 1857 or India's First War of Independence. None are satisfactory titles.

The trigger for this uprising was misunderstanding and rumour. The new Pattern 1853 Enfield rifle fired Minié balls and used paper cartridges that came pre-greased. To load the rifle, a soldier would have to bite the cartridge open to release the powder. This was a simple way to speed up the process of loading. However, the grease used on these cartridges included tallow (from beef), which would be offensive to Hindu soldiers (Sepoys), or lard (from pork), which would be offensive to Muslim soldiers.

When the difficulties were pointed out, the matter was quickly resolved with the use of vegetable grease instead. This is an example of imperial sensitivity to local customs and culture, but that's not the way it is remembered. Instead, when the original information reached Mangal Pandey, a Sepoy, he was so incensed that he fired at his lieutenant, luckily missing the man but hitting his horse. Then he tried to get his fellow soldiers to rise up, but nobody was really interested. So, to avoid imprisonment (for insurrection), Pandey chose to become a martyr, placed a musket to his chest and pulled the trigger with his toe. However, he managed only to wound himself and was court-martialled for his trouble.

Pandey's regiment was disbanded and stripped of their uniforms because it was felt that they harboured ill-feelings towards their superiors, which was demonstrably not true, and Sepoys in other regiments thought this as a very harsh punishment. It is more likely that this action, rather than the greased cartridge episode, was the provocation that caused out-of-work soldiers to rise up.

Accounts of what happened next depend on whether you're Indian or British – both are politically charged. The ill-disciplined Indian rebels looked for soft targets, and there's no denying that defenceless British families were massacred more often than soldiers in pitched battles. These instances of outrage against civilians led to brutal suppression by the forces of the East India Company, which wanted, at times, little more than revenge. In the end far more Indians died than Brits, a fact no one disputes. However, vast areas of India actually sided with the East India Company or were largely neutral in their views. These were not the birth cries of Indian independence ... yet.

From the point of view of Parliament, enough was enough. The possession of a country the size of India shouldn't be in the hands of a company. The East India Company was disbanded and control of India transferred to the British Crown. Shortly after this, the last Mughal emperor died, so ending a dynasty that had ruled immense parts of India (including modern Pakistan) for centuries. In 1877 (as advised by Prime Minister Benjamin Disraeli) Queen Victoria became Empress of India, the first imperial title of the British Empire.

60. Britain and Russia Played a Great Game

As the British Empire moved out of the sub-continent and further into Asia, there was another empire to worry about – Russia. Just as Britain had been expanding its dominions over the continents of the world, Russia had been building an empire of its own. Huge swathes of Asia that had been the traditional strongholds of Tartar or Mongol warlords were brought to heel by Peter the Great.

The nineteenth century was an era when these two great empires vied for any kind of advantage over exotic and remote lands such as Afghanistan. This period of diplomatic and sometimes military manoeuvring was referred to as 'The Great Game'.

In 1838 Britain launched a war with Afghanistan to install a puppet regime. This was subsequently named the First Anglo-Afghan War. It eventually ended in a massacre of all British civilians and all but one member of the British forces. That man was a doctor, allowed to live to tell the terrible tale that was meant to keep the British out.

In 1877, the Russians re-ran the Crimean War against their long-standing enemy, the now weakened Ottoman Empire. Russia had cleverly isolated the Ottomans diplomatically, so, when war broke out, France and Britain had no legitimate reason to interfere. When the Ottomans lost, Russia was able to gain political sway in the Balkans and the Caucuses, the repercussions of which are still being felt to this day.

The Russians continued to increase their power in central Asia until 1878, when the Second Anglo-Afghan War took place. The Brits had learned from their mistakes. This war involved constant movement and was a military operation only (no baggage trains full of wives and children). And this time it managed the successful establishment of a puppet regime in Afghanistan, making it a buffer between the two great empires.

By the 1890s, competition for land had moved even further east into Tibet and China as the two empires continued to bump into each other. Persia (modern Iran) was another example of a once powerful empire which had atrophied through time and then had to deal with interference from Russia and Britain. It was an intense situation for such nations: which side to trust? What if the opposing side gained the upper hand?

Like a surprising amount of imperial disputes in the age of empire, matters were eventually resolved through diplomacy and the signing of an agreement. This was called the Anglo-Russian Convention of 1907 and set in stone the zones of influence and the national boundaries that identified respective control in areas such as Persia, Afghanistan and Tibet.

It was an example of that most imperial of ideas – a 'gentleman's agreement'. While this agreement was to affect millions of people, it did reduce, rather than increase, the need for conflict.

61. A Girl Named George Made Literary History

Male pseudonyms were frequently used by four of Britain's greatest writers. Because there is no denying that the patriarchal society of the nineteenth century limited even fundamental options for women, it is remarkable that some of the greatest writers in the English language are the women of this era, who were able to get their books published and sold them by the cart load.

Even though she only just scrapes into the nineteenth century, first mention must be made of Jane Austin, who wrote many novels (most notably, *Sense and Sensibility* and *Pride and Prejudice*) and early on wrote anonymously as 'A Lady'. One of the most widely read of any English writers, her books are historically significant for their social commentary. Although her work enjoyed some contemporary popularity, she never achieved personal fame and was not recognised as a great English writer until the 1940s.

The Brontë sisters came from Haworth in Yorkshire and wrote such greats as *Wuthering Heights* (Emily) and *Jane Eyre* (Charlotte). Anne died at twenty-nine, having written two novels: *Agnes Grey* and *The Tenant of Wildfell Hall*. Eventually the Brontës became successful enough to drop their masculine pseudonyms and reveal their true identities. Their brother was also literary but lapsed into alcoholism and laudanum addiction. It's nothing less than tragic that all six Brontë siblings were dead by thirty-eight (two sisters died in childhood). Their personal stories are sobering reminders of how brutal life could be for all but the richest in the nineteenth century.

Mary Ann Evans, known by the pen name of George Eliot, lived into her sixties and was able to accumulate a large body of work, but it was her later novels, *Silas Marner* and *Middlemarch*, which are considered to be her greatest works. *Middlemarch* was revolutionary in that it was the name of a fictional town, so instead of a central character, it has multiple plots and a large cast of characters, linked through distinct, interlocking narratives.

Evans became famous enough to have used her own name, but she chose not to do so because she didn't want her complex works to be pigeonholed with the light romances of some other women writers.

In terms of the significance of their books, these women might justifiably claim to be the most important female writers in British history, but there was another who beat them all. Indeed, in terms of sales, she beats everyone. Agatha Christie (1890–1976) wrote over seventy novels and short story collections. Ironically, she sometimes used a pen name too, but she chose a female one – Mary Westmacott. Her crime fiction is still wildly popular and her play *The Mousetrap* is the longest running play in history. It opened in 1952 and plays somewhere in the world every day. Her novels have sold roughly 4 billion copies.

Imperial Britain could be justifiably proud of the fact that its readers were open-minded enough to embrace these literary works, irrespective of gender.

62. IMPERIAL INVENTION NO. 5: EVOLUTION

Most scientific books are read by only a few people. In rare instances, some of these books enter the public domain and become part of our broader understanding of science and nature. However, one book has not only never been out of print in the last 150 years, but also has triggered major theological arguments. Written by an ex–medical student and first published in 1859, the book in question is *On the Origin of Species* by Charles Darwin.

Most of Darwin's books were on very dry subjects as perfectly demonstrated by his last work *The Formation of Vegetable Mould through the Action of Worms* (this was not a best seller). It certainly was never Darwin's intention to court controversy. His ideas about evolution evolved (a-hem) beyond his own writings until phrases like 'Social Darwinism', which became synonymous with thinly veiled racism, were unjustly associated with a charming and kind-hearted family man who, at times, played musical instruments to pots of earthworms.

The sheer genius of *On the Origin of the Species* is its elegance and simplicity. Unlike the worlds of chemistry or physics, the idea needs no mathematics to understand it. Contrary to common perception, it is not the fittest that thrive (according to the theory), but those species that can adapt to changing environments. If, for example, over a period of time, the shell of a nut becomes thicker, then the birds with larger beaks will be able to crack through the nut. The birds with smaller beaks will have to find another food source, and so, over many generations, what had once been one species becomes two. It is a very simple way of explaining the myriad varieties of life on earth. In the original book Darwin talked exclusively about animal evolution, leaving the reader to draw his own conclusions about how humans fit into all of this.

The idea of evolution began to emerge during Darwin's famous voyage on the *Beagle*, which took him, for the most part, to the southern hemisphere. However, it was not until twenty years after this voyage that he felt he had enough evidence to prove his theory and the conviction to make it public.

Once an idea is in print, it is impossible to suppress. The theory of evolution eliminates the need for a creator and is in direct contrast to the early verses in the Book of Genesis. However, by the 1870s, most people (including liberal Anglican clerics) who knew of the idea accepted evolution. It's a sad fact that religious fundamentalists have tried hard to push back against the idea in recent decades, and the arguments have polarised between science and religion. While this debate continues to rumble on, the majority of scientists today would agree that Darwin got it right.

63. EUROPE CARVED UP THE DARK CONTINENT

In 1870 roughly 10 per cent of Africa was under imperial rule by one of the European empires. It's a stark and stunning fact that by 1914 that had increased to 90 per cent. The remaining 10 per cent was composed of just two countries: Liberia, which had been created as a colony for ex-slaves, and Abyssinia (modern Ethiopia), which had resisted all invasion attempts.

In the space of forty years, hundreds of thousands of square miles of a continent had traded local overlords for imperial ones. This could never have happened had the grandiose ambitions of these competing empires been at odds. Instead, the carving up of Africa is another example of decisions taken by a committee of gentlemen in the drawing rooms of Europe; in this case, decisions which led to huge upheavals for the natives of another continent.

The redrawing of the African political map became known as the 'Scramble for Africa'. Of course, the locals didn't realise that Germany or Britain now 'owned' their land in a period of colonialism that saw some of the most one-sided victories in imperial history. Cecil Rhodes is the perfect example of someone who orchestrated a war. In 1893 he picked a fight with the Matabele because he wanted the raw materials these natives were sitting on. Although his 1,000 troops fought an army of 100,000, there was never any contest. The Matabele had cowhide shields and spears, while Rhodes had belt-fed machine guns. It was hardly a war, more a genocide. Cecil's new lands were called Rhodesia.

The newly arrived 'German Empire' was also looking for a place in the sun but had to accept that France and Britain had first claims to the continent because of the size of their existing empires. There is a probably apocryphal story that Queen Victoria took pity on Kaiser Wilhelm II (one of her grandsons) and in 1886, simply by arbitrarily changing borders, gave him Mount Kilimanjaro as a birthday present. Even though this kind of breathtakingly blasé attitude stopped a European war, it showed a total lack of regard for native populations and no understanding of the political and cultural realities on the ground.

The Zulu Wars, with the famous British defeat at the Battle of Isandlwana and the even more famous victory at Rorke's Drift, both happened in 1879. They are just two examples of dozens of colonial campaigns fought by Belgians, Italians, French, Germans and Brits, all turning a theoretical map into reality. They were also the last great spasms of growth in the European empires. Therefore, it is ironic that this era has coloured most people's perceptions of 'empire'. For every negative image, there is an exotic one of intrepid explorers clad in khaki and pith helmets. Relatively speaking, this was a short period in imperial history and certainly was not the experience (either positive or negative) of most of the inhabitants of the British Empire.

64. CHARLES GORDON WAS AN IMPERIAL MARTYR

Charles Gordon was everything you would expect from a Victorian gentleman. He had long sideburns, a strong chin and an even stronger sense of self-importance. He was a good military tactician and he was brave. He had served with honour in the British Army in the Crimean War and as the leader of a Chinese contingent in the Taiping Rebellion. His military and imperial credentials were impeccable.

After fighting off rebels, Gordon became the governor-general of the Sudan in the 1870s. He also stopped the local slave trade, which was the morally right thing to do, but which caused a recession in Sudan, where the slave trade had been an important source of income.

By 1880 Gordon had had enough adventure and retired to Britain (via China, where he stopped a war between China and Russia. Honestly, the man was a dynamo). He had achieved everything any man could have hoped for in one lifetime.

However, back in Sudan, an Islamic fundamentalist uprising was taking place. This was led by the enigmatic Muhammad Ahmad, who had declared himself the Mahdi (according to Islamic tradition, the redeemer of Islam). When the situation in the Sudan was assumed to be lost, the authorities planned to evacuate the British and Egyptian imperial staff (and their families) back to the safety of Egypt. Gordon was asked to go to Khartoum to oversee the evacuation. How could he turn down such a call for help?

But once in Khartoum, Gordon started to believe his own hype and against orders, set up an HQ, which he defended against Mahdist forces. By March 1884, the

Muslims had Khartoum surrounded, but Gordon kept his head, betting that the British would send a relief force. Parliament, however, dithered, and it wasn't until August that a 'flying' column of cavalry (on camels) was dispatched.

The force didn't reach the Sudan until January of 1885. Gordon was still hanging on, so the force moved further south, now supported by the gunboats that Gordon had sent up the Nile for rendezvous. The relief army arrived two days too late. The Mahdist forces had only just captured Khartoum, and Gordon, along with 10,000 civilians, had died in the last battle.

His death was felt across the empire. Gordon of Khartoum was Victorian imperialism personified in one man. For a decade the British had to admit the loss of control of the Sudan to Mahdist forces. However, in the late 1890s, under General Kitchener, a sizeable British force arrived in Khartoum and defeated the Mahdists. In 1898, the Anglo-Egyptian force fought the Battle of Omdurman, which was to be the last British imperial cavalry charge (one of the soldiers in it was a young Winston Churchill). The Mahdists were shattered, and Muhammad Ahmad was killed shortly afterwards (his passing was not mourned by the Sudanese), effectively ending the Mahdist era and restoring British rule to the Sudan.

65. GLADSTONE AND DISRAELI DEFINED VICTORIAN POLITICS

'Ladies and gentlemen, tonight we present a special match. In the red corner, the four times Chancellor of the Exchequer and four times Liberal Prime Minister – William Ewart Gladstone! And in the blue corner (literally), the two times prime minister, founder of the Conservative Party and the only Jewish prime minister in British history – Benjamin Disraeli!'

If two politicians were to define the Victorian era, then these would be the ones. They were both great statesmen, but they loathed each other, and their rivalry personified the anxieties of imperial rule. The nineteenth century had its fair share of influential statesmen: William Pitt the Younger didn't get a mention in the Napoleonic Wars, but it was his sterling efforts that saved Britain every bit as much as those of Nelson and Wellington. However, it was the late nineteenth century, with the various reform Acts broadening the interest of politics to the wider electorate, which encompassed these two men, their battles against each other and their attempts to appeal to the masses.

Disraeli loved the affairs of empire. He was the prime minister who recognised that the Suez Canal was a lifeline for British interests in India and bought the French share (controversially, with the help of a Rothschild's fortune and not the Bank of England). It was also Disraeli who encouraged Queen Victoria to take the title of Empress of India. Disraeli understood *realpolitik*, the reality of a situation, and used it to his advantage.

Less interested in imperial affairs, Gladstone was a Liberal and a staunch Christian, who always had one eye on moral issues. This was a prime minister who attempted to rescue and rehabilitate prostitutes. For decades, he walked the streets of London to encourage working girls to find more honest forms of employment. Although he was criticised for this behaviour, nobody seriously suggested that he might have a hidden agenda for his late-night activities. With regard to empire, he was the prime minister who created momentum behind the idea of 'home rule'. While this was framed in paternalistic tones, it was a sign that Britain wanted to work in partnership with its myriad empire lands, rather than as a dictator, as so many other empires did.

In their own ways, both men fought for the literal heart and soul of the empire, making the British Empire an unusual mix of tolerance and harmony, as well as racism and belligerence. Gladstone was, in some respects, the more modern of the two. He was worried about the effects of British power on overseas peoples. He was often apologetic and able to temper potential excesses. But Disraeli had a gift for connecting with the common man. He was less morally judgmental and a lot more practical than Gladstone.

The two often exchanged barbed comments in the Houses of Parliament and in public speeches; however, it was this spark and fire that indicated Parliamentary democracy was alive and well in the United Kingdom.

66. James Clark Maxwell Is a Forgotten Genius

James Clark Maxwell is probably not a name you know; however, this Scottish scientist was the most gifted physicist after Newton and before Einstein.

Since this is a history book, there is probably no need for an in-depth study of kinetic theory and thermodynamics ... which is a good thing as I can't write one. However, through his study of optics, Maxwell was able to produce practical colour photography, which, while impressive, was the least of his legacy. His work on electromagnetism resulted in the first accurate measurement of the speed of light and also predicted the existence of radio waves. He even proved Saturn's rings were made out of particles and were not solid.

Maxwell's potential was recognised from an early age; he wrote his first scientific paper at the age of fourteen. He spent his academic career shifting among the cream of English and Scottish educational centres where he conducted his research and wrote extensively of his findings. He died from abdominal cancer in 1879 at the age of forty-eight.

Maxwell's work is so important, complex and influential that it's difficult to simplify, but he is generally recognised as the 'father of modern physics'. By way of summary, it's useful to note what others have said: 'Maxwell's achievements concerning electromagnetism have been called the second great unification in physics after the first one realised by Isaac Newton.' Perhaps more significantly, Maxwell was one of Einstein's heroes; and praise doesn't come much higher than that.

67. Isambard Kingdom Brunel Was the Engineer of the British Empire

If there is one man who both looked and acted the part of a Victorian engineer, it has to be Isambard Kingdom Brunel. He was actually dead by the late nineteenth century, but his legacy has survived him for decades.

Somewhat surprisingly, Brunel wasn't quite as British as you might think: his father was French and his early education was in France. A smart and capable student, he had mastered Euclidean geometry, as taught to him by his father, by the age of eight.

Brunel's first major engineering work was in collaboration with his father, who engineered the building of the Thames Tunnel, a highly complicated project and the first ever tunnel to be completed under a navigable river. His first solo project (when he was just twenty-five) was the Clifton Suspension Bridge, which was, at the time, the longest suspension bridge in the world. However, there were major delays, and while the bridge that still exists today is his design, it wasn't finally completed until five years after his death.

Many of Brunel's projects bankrupted investors or ended up not being fully adopted. An example was his broad-gauge Great Western Railway. The railway required a seven-foot-wide track, which Brunel had calculated would make the most comfortable journey for passengers. However, if the width of the gauges wasn't built to a single agreed standard, it would mean goods and passengers would have to be moved to a new train for a different gauge of track. Brunel's idea was abandoned as impractical.

Brunel seemed to think that every problem could be solved by engineering. On one occasion he swallowed a half sovereign at a children's party. The coin lodged in his lung, and there was a genuine danger of complications from this accidental ingestion. No problem. Brunel simply (and quickly) concocted a table that could pivot him upside down. He reasoned gravity would dislodge the troublesome coin, and to everyone's relief, it did!

During the Crimean War, he invented what was essentially a flat pack hospital, which proved to be highly successful, thanks mainly to the fact that it was easy to assemble. However, it is in the realms of shipping that Brunel really made his mark. In 1843 he completed the SS *Great Britain*, the first propeller-driven, ocean-going iron ship. Although this was not the first ever screw propeller driven ship, the vast majority of steam-powered ships used the far less efficient paddle-wheel system. At 322 feet, it was also a monster, the largest ship ever built at the time. The six-blade propeller, which produced speeds of up to eleven knots, was so well designed that modern computer models can only fractionally improve its efficiency. Its reputation as the first 'modern' ship is truly justified.

Brunel was only one of many designers and engineers of the era, but with his grandiose plans, his staggering talent and his trademark stovepipe hat and cigar, he was the very epitome of a Victorian engineer.

68. Imperial Invention No. 6: Christmas

When Mount Tambora in Indonesia erupted in 1815, it knocked the entire world's weather system out of balance. This event did not make the British papers, and yet its repercussions would have a significant impact on British culture, indeed, on world culture. Because of this eruption, Britain would have abnormally harsh winters for the next several years. This meant snow at Christmas, which was unusual in England. For one four-year-old boy, this phenomenon would prove to be a seminal experience because, for the first few Christmases that he could remember, they were snowy and magical.

Because his father was locked up in a debtor's prison, the boy had a tough upbringing and was forced, at one point, to work in a factory. His was educated in a rather average school, but he was bright and later started to work as a junior clerk in a law office. Thanks to family connections, he was able to move from there to a career in journalism. This gave him the opportunity to publish his short stories, which were later serialised in newspapers.

This is the story of Charles Dickens, Britain's greatest writer, second only to Shakespeare. His books are classics, still selling well and continuing to entertain us today. *A Tale of Two Cities*, *Oliver Twist*, *Great Expectations* and *The Old Curiosity Shop* are a few of his best known works. His formative years of poverty and harsh living are to be found in these pages of literary perfection. However, it was another masterpiece, *A Christmas Carol*, which is pivotal to the story of Christmas. As our contemporary Western European Christmas traditions all come from the pages of Dickens's book, Christmases in the eighteenth century and earlier would have looked very different to anything we know today.

The story takes place in an unusually snowy London, which recalls Dickens' childhood memories. Exchanging presents, roasting a large bird, eating Christmas pudding – putting all these together was a surprisingly novel idea. In 1843, the book's year of publication, Sir Henry Cole made and sent the very first Christmas cards. The German tradition of the Christmas tree had only recently been introduced to Britain by Prince Albert, but by 1842 there were adverts for them in the London papers.

A goose was then the most common bird to be served for the Christmas meal. While turkeys had been in Britain since the sixteenth century, they only became popular holiday eating much later in the nineteenth century. Christmas celebrations had, for centuries, been nothing like anything the first Christians would have recognised, but these earlier festivities would have been alien to us too. In just a few short years in the Victorian era, the Christmas celebrations we recognise today were brought together.

So, it's probably fair to say that modern Christmas celebrations have more to do with Victorian England than first-century Palestine.

69. THE WHITECHAPEL MURDERS GAVE BIRTH TO TABLOID JOURNALISM

In 1888 in the Whitechapel area of London, vulnerable poor women were being murdered. Their bodies were horrifically mutilated by an unknown assailant(s). It's not even clear how many women were murdered by the same serial killer(s) or even when the killing ended.

All of this is worth mentioning because as soon as anyone says, 'Jack the Ripper', heads fill with preconceptions. The earliest eyewitness accounts describe men in the area as plainly or shabbily dressed. Some suspected there were several men working together (hence, all the (s)es). The idea of a gentleman serial killer, in a top hat and cape, is a twentieth-century construct, usually a metaphor for the rich being able to do whatever they liked to the poor. They, literally, got away with murder. That was not the tone of the reporting at the time, but that's not to say the reporting of the time was particularly sober.

As modern forensics indicate that at least five of the women were the victims of the same man (or men), other victims in the period 1888–1891 were probably murdered by different killers. Beyond sensational headlines, this string of murders is notable for the birth of two modern phenomena: investigative policing and tabloid journalism.

Professional policemen (another British invention) had been around for over twenty years, but they were still a fairly rudimentary force. While the 'Whitechapel murders' are certainly not the first example of serial killing, they were the first to be widely publicised and, because of the circumstances, required the gathering of evidence, an understanding of clues and an appreciation of psychology. However, at the time, investigators were so stumped for clues that photographs were taken of the victims' eyes as there was an old wives' tale that the image of the murderer would remain in the pupils. This was the last era of superstition and science mixing together – and the very start of investigative police work.

And it wasn't just police work which was evolving. Although this was a time of press freedom, the Whitechapel murders are the first example of murder stories selling newspapers. Perjury is a serious crime; financial mismanagement can affect thousands, but if you want to sell more copies of your paper, put a gruesome murder on the front page.

It is a slightly disturbing human trait that we love reading about the dark acts of fellow humans, so even though the killings shocked, they also generated enormous interest. Because newspapers competed to report the most lurid details, we can trace the rise of tabloid journalism back to these murders.

To add to the sensationalism of the crimes and to seal their fame, the murderer(s) was never caught, which allows conspiracy theories to continue to flourish. The killer's name is unlikely to have been Jack, but Jack the Ripper is a name as famous as Sherlock Holmes.

70. A Victorian Almost Invented the Computer

If Britain's empire was a maritime power, then it needed a timetable. How long would rubber from South East Asia take to get to Liverpool? When would the mechanical parts sent from Newcastle arrive in Gibraltar? Although maritime tables had long been around, human errors crept in. Inaccuracies slowed the flow of trade, which led to stockpiles in some ports and deficits in others. If only there was a way to eliminate human error.

In 1822 Charles Babbage (an engineer and inventor) proposed the creation of a mechanical device that could flawlessly compute maritime tables. Powered by hand cranking, this machine was called a 'difference engine' and used the novel decimal number system for calculations. At this point, the difference engine was only a theory, but the British government was interested and gave Babbage £1,700, then a significant sum of money, to start work on the project.

Babbage's design was all about precision, starting with the parts needed to make it. Nobody had built to such meticulous standards before, and while it was possible, the work was costly and time consuming. Twenty years later, Babbage had spent £17,000 (then the cost of a battleship) and still didn't have a completed difference engine to show for his efforts. As the original idea had been to build a machine that could quickly and cheaply produce better maritime tables, it was shelved. However, what Babbage had almost invented was a working mechanical computer.

71. IMPERIAL INVENTION No. 7:
THE MACHINE GUN

Hiram Maxim was, in some ways, a man of his time and, in others, an anomaly. Through reason and observation he became an atheist – not an uncommon philosophical journey in the Victorian era. He also concluded (not unreasonably) that Christian missionary work in China was causing more harm than good. Hiram was unusual in that he was American-born and immigrated to Britain (aged forty-one) at a time when most immigrants were going the other way, but he earned his living in that most Victorian of ways, as an inventor and engineer.

Hiram took great interest in the more lethal side of inventions. By the 1880s firearms had developed into far more efficient weapons than their early nineteenth-century counterparts. Instead of taking half a minute to reload, the new self-contained, metal-encased bullets meant much faster firing, and the development of smokeless powder (another Maxim invention) meant the shooter could not be easily located by the tell-tale puff of smoke. Rifles also had greatly improved accuracy and could now kill men from half a mile away (as recently as the Crimean War, it took luck to fire two rounds per minute and hit anything further away than 100 yards). Most of these innovations had nothing to do with Maxim, but he pulled them all together in one terrifying gun.

What Maxim invented in 1884 was a machine with a canvas belt of bullets that fed into a new type of gun. After the round was fired, energy from the recoil was used to push the spent casing out of the gun and pull the next round into the barrel where the process would begin again. No need for cocking, priming or working the bolt. After pulling the trigger, the gun kept firing until it ran out of bullets. The Maxim gun was the world's first fully automatic portable machine gun.

Being able to fire 500–600 rounds a minute meant that four of these two-man machines could do the work of several companies of soldiers. What was worse was that when they were put in the field against massed ranks of native tribes, the result was like cutting butter with a hot knife, only in this instance, the hot knife was a gun that led to the deaths of thousands of brave warriors, who stood no chance against such a machine.

This first machine gun was Maxim's gift to his new country, and he was rewarded with a knighthood. The gun was mass produced in Britain by Vickers and became known as the Vickers heavy machine gun. It had such an unfair advantage in imperial conquest (particularly in Africa) that the poet Hilaire Belloc mentioned it in his poem *The Modern Traveller*: 'Whatever happens, we have got / The Maxim gun, and they have not.' However, the time was fast approaching when both sides would have this terrifyingly efficient weapon.

72. The Rothschilds Combined Decadence and Philanthropy

The village of Waddesdon in Buckinghamshire is pleasant but unremarkable and not worth a special visit ... except that is, for a gigantic Neo-Renaissance style French château called Waddesdon Manor. It looks old, but a plaque reveals that the manor was built in the late nineteenth century. This is a palace, not for a monarch, but for the businessman Baron Ferdinand de Rothschild.

The Rothschilds were a Jewish family from Frankfurt, who, over the late eighteenth and early nineteenth centuries, built a powerful banking empire. The family illustrates the reality that although the age of empire may have been about war and the acquisition of exotic lands, it was also about business, and the Rothschilds were second to none when it came to spotting lucrative opportunities. Of course, money only went so far in Victorian society, and even though Ferdinand was a baron, he didn't have the stately home or castle he thought befitted his position. Waddesdon was his very successful attempt to give the family some heritage and status.

The British branch of the family had been intertwined with British imperial interests for generations. The bank provided funds for the armies of the Duke of Wellington in Portugal and Spain in the early nineteenth century. Later, in 1875, Lionel de Rothschild financed the British government's purchase of the Suez Canal. He was also the first practicing Jew to become an MP.

It is estimated that the family (including the European branches) fortune was around £200 billion, but comparing worth in one age with that in another is always tricky. It's fair to say this was one of the richest non-royal dynasties in history.

Although much of the family's money was tied up in land, assets, industrial schemes and projects like the Suez Canal, there was plenty to spare. The baron was not averse to indulging himself, and he knew how to throw a party. In fact, Waddesdon was never used as a residence – it was kept as a party house (this was not a problem because the family had at least ten other homes in south-east England alone). At one dinner party there were pythons wrapped around the staircase, zebras roaming the grounds and a chimpanzee who dined with the guests.

But the Rothschilds were also great philanthropists. They funded hospitals, educational centres and numerous charities, while their donations of works of art to galleries around the world are the largest of any family in history.

A little like the British Empire itself, what made this edifice of financial invulnerability wobble was the huge death toll and enormous financial cost of the First World War, and later, the persecution of Jews across Europe in the Second World War.

The Rothschild family is still with us, still funding philanthropic projects ('It's in our DNA,' says the current patriarch), but the family's glory days are behind them. Even though it is still undeniably wealthy, they aren't nearly as rich, powerful or well-connected as they once were.

73. Queen Victoria's Heirs Ruled Europe

Victoria and Albert were married for twenty-one years before Albert's sudden death from typhoid fever at the age of just forty-two. The couple had nine children. Her eldest daughter (also Victoria) had eight children, and in total, the queen was grandmother to forty grandchildren.

Victoria loved Albert deeply, and when he died in 1861 (the same year as her mother) she went into mourning and withdrew from public life. Some dubbed her the 'Widow of Windsor', and while she never stopped grieving for her dear Albert, she had been preparing for the future.

Her plan was to marry off her children to the great houses of Europe to ensure cooperation in the future. It was a good plan, and three of her grandchildren were to become very grand indeed. The aforementioned eldest daughter, Victoria, married into the Prussian royal family; her first-born child was to become Kaiser Wilhelm II. Tsar Nicholas II was also a grandson on his mother's side. King George V of Britain, who ruled from 1910, was another grandson. By the outbreak of the First World War, three of the grandchildren were a tsar, a kaiser and an emperor, probably making Queen Victoria the greatest matriarch in history.

There were some interesting similarities and differences among these three rulers. The most obvious physical likeness was between Nicholas and George, who looked so remarkably similar that they occasionally dressed in each other's clothes as a joke. However, beneath the familial fun, there were major differences in power. On paper, George V was emperor of the largest empire the world had ever seen and should have had enough power to make Caesar Augustus green with envy, but instead he was a figurehead. The real power lay with Parliament.

Contrast King George's position with those of his two cousins, Tsar Nicholas and the Kaiser Wilhelm: these two men were absolute monarchs. Individually they had far more power, but their nations were envious of Britain. Russia had recently abolished serfdom, but in many ways it was still a largely agrarian, semi-feudal society. In the very early twentieth century, the country was humiliated by Japan in a brief but emphatic war, making Russia the first European power to be humbled by an Asian one.

Germany was a new country and late to the game of empire. Even though it had shamed its old enemy France in the Franco-Prussian War of 1870–1, it was very much the junior empire builder and looked on enviously at the British dominions protected by the world's mightiest navy. The Royal Navy became an obsession with Germany, and it was clear that an arms race was developing between two countries that had been allies.

When war was looming in 1914, the three did try to communicate with each other in order to avert global conflict, but not even these hugely powerful men could stop Europe from descending into chaos – and at least one of them actively encouraged it.

74. IMPERIAL INVENTION No. 8: THE SUBWAY

Known to locals as 'the tube', the London subway system was the world's first underground passenger railway. As London turned into the world's largest city, the growing population needed to find an affordable way to move around and get to work. Carriages were expensive and bicycles were impractical. Perhaps inspired by Brunel's Thames Tunnel, the authorities came up with the idea of an underground train.

It was all very experimental, and digging through London clay had its problems, but in 1863 the world's first underground railway was opened between Paddington and Farringdon. The first generation of trains was grim. The wooden carriages were gas-lit (no danger of anything going wrong with that) and pulled by steam engines. The dirt and soot must have been stifling. But the concept was a great success, and ten years later, there were thirty stations spread across the city. Thankfully, in 1890, electric trains were introduced, and the network continued to grow. Probably its most unforeseen use was as an air raid shelter in the First World War and, again, during the Blitz in the Second World War.

It was Harry Beck, in 1931, who developed the famous schematic tube map. He realised that travellers on the tube did not need to know directions or distances as much as they needed to understand where they were and how to get to their destinations. Both the tube, as a transit system, and Beck's iconic map have inspired imitations around the world.

75. The Diamond Jubilee Was the Best Empire Party Ever

In 1896 Queen Victoria became the longest reigning monarch in British history; however, she wanted to delay any celebrations until 1897 so that they could coincide with her Diamond Jubilee. The scene was set for an empire to celebrate its global achievements.

The high point was to be a procession through London on 22 June. The preceding days were a whirlwind of meetings and banquets with over fifty kings, queens and heads of state. Less exalted leaders, as well as the prime ministers of the semi-independent dominions (such as Canada) also attended as pretty much everyone wanted to be part of this unique moment in history. Hundreds of thousands congregated in London; nobody knows the exact figure, but it wouldn't be a wild exaggeration to say that the numbers reached half a million. Thousands slept overnight in the parks to ensure a good spot for the parade.

By now the British Empire had a presence on virtually every continent and covered roughly 25 per cent of the world's landmass. As a quarter of the global population was under British rule, literally hundreds of different races and cultures were represented in the exotic diversity which symbolised imperial power.

22 June 1897 was a typical British summer's day: overcast with a chance of showers. However, the skies cleared, and the day became progressively sunnier, matching the mood of the crowds. Victoria had signalled the start of the celebrations with a telegraph message, the very latest in modern communications, while the procession itself was announced with cannon fire. The colourful seventeen-carriage convoy was

interspersed with every conceivable variety of cavalry that the empire encompassed. Policemen in their darkest blue and British soldiers resplendent in their bright red jackets lined the six-mile route. The streets were crammed with joyous crowds, waving flags and cheering the procession.

It's remarkable that this Victorian era, which seems so foreign to our own times, was recent enough to have been filmed. Even though the black and white recording is silent, the sheer vibrancy and enthusiasm of the day pours out of the grainy footage. It captures a time gone by, but it was clearly one of the greatest parties any empire had ever seen.

In her journal the queen wrote, 'No one ever, I believe, has met with such an ovation as was given to me, passing through those 6 miles of streets ... The cheering was quite deafening & every face seemed to be filled with real joy. I was much moved and gratified.'

It is the first example of the empire coming to Britain, and it was a dazzling display of confidence and success. Victoria may not have had much in the way of genuine power, but she personified the age, and as the frail, seventy-eight-year-old monarch waved to the exuberant crowds, in some symbolic way this procession marked the very apogee of the British Empire.

76. The British Empire Was an Imperial Bully in South Africa

In 1880 Britain had attempted to annexe South Africa and failed, but the lure of substantial deposits in the Witwatersrand gold mines and the Kimberley diamond mines was too great to resist. The riches were just over the border from British territory and were protected by only a few thousand white (Boer) farmers. Why not take them? This (technically second) Boer War was about greed, pure and simple.

From 1899–1902 Britain fought this war of aggression against fewer than 100,000 irregular Boer fighters. Initially the Boers outmanoeuvred the British and besieged them in key sites, most famously at Ladysmith. That siege lasted over three months and was a rare example of British forces being outnumbered by the Boers, who then had the advantage with the latest rifles, artillery and machine guns supplied by the famous German Krupp munitions factory. General Buller's relief force (which had Winston Churchill in the column) broke the siege for the British in late February of 1900.

After a year's fighting, little had been achieved except for casualties and the subsequent need for a mass injection of troops. The Boers, however, had no such luxury of reserves. Ignorant of the steam roller heading their way, the Boers were able to inflict a humiliating defeat at Spion Kop, where their artillery tore into poorly placed British positions (Gandhi was a stretcher bearer in this battle). When a huge army of British reinforcements arrived, it swept into Boer-held territory and captured Pretoria, their capital. At its peak the British had about half a million men fighting in South Africa.

After this, the Boer forces drifted away into the immense African interior where they split into small 'commando' groups designed for hit and run raids. It was classic guerrilla warfare.

Now led by General Kitchener, the British responded with one good idea and another cruel one. They created a network of some 8,000 blockhouses, tiny fortified outposts manned by a handful of men, built so that the Boer commandos could be spotted and tracked. In the event of an attack, the blockhouses were a safe haven.

The cruel plan was also a criminal act. Boer families were rounded up and sent to prison camps called concentration camps. Later on, the Nazis were to make much of the fact that the British had invented these, and although their purpose had been imprisonment rather than death, conditions were such that people were dying ... in their thousands. When news of this reached Britain, there was a cry of outrage. Britain wanted to win but not at any cost, and this was clearly an immoral act.

The blockhouses and concentration camps were the last straw for the exhausted Boers, and they capitulated to British rule in 1902. This is a clear example of the 'bad guys' winning a war. Of all the imperial conflicts between 1815 and 1914, the Boer War was the longest and bloodiest.

77. The Seeds of the First World War Were Sewn in Morocco

The seeds of the First World War were not sewn in Serbia in 1914, but a decade earlier ... in Morocco.

Prior to the start of the First World War, two events show that even though there was an international willingness to threaten, most wanted to avoid actual conflict. These largely forgotten crises reveal the simmering rivalries between European powers, and although the situations were resolved peacefully, the cost was one of considerable resentment. These diplomatic spats were known as the First and Second Moroccan Crisis.

Global imperial politics of the nineteenth and early twentieth century were about as complex as they could be, but I will try to keep things simple. In 1905 there was a diplomatic row over the status of Morocco. Germany attempted to use the issue of Morocco's independence not only to increase frictions between France and Britain, but also to advance its own commercial interests by supporting the country's new status. While Germany ultimately succeeded in assuring that independence, it failed to attract international diplomatic support for its position. The crisis resulted in a deterioration of Germany's relations with both France and Britain, helping to ensure the success of the new Anglo-French 'Entente Cordiale'.

As Britain had defended France diplomatically against Germany, the First Moroccan Crisis showed that the Entente Cordiale was more than just words. But Kaiser Wilhelm II was angry over being politically outmanoeuvred, and that made him feel even more insecure than before. Wilhelm was determined not to back down again, which led to the German involvement in the Second Moroccan Crisis six years later.

The new crisis occurred in April of 1911, when France broke the terms that had been agreed at the end of the first dispute by sending troops into Morocco to 'keep the peace' and protect French interests. Germany reacted by sending a gunboat to the port of Agadir to protect Moroccan independence. The German response provoked the British as they thought that the Germans meant to turn Agadir into a naval base on the Atlantic coast. As far as the Royal Navy was concerned, this would give the Germans unacceptable access to the Atlantic shipping lanes.

However, in the middle of this second crisis, Germany was hit by financial turmoil when the stock market plunged by 30 per cent in a single day. Faced with the likelihood of being forced to abandon the gold standard, the kaiser backed down and let the French take over most of Morocco. France subsequently established a full protectorate over the country, bringing to an end what remained of its brief independence. Instead of scaring Britain into turning towards Germany, the chief result had been to increase British fear and hostility and to draw Britain closer to France. The kaiser's plan had backfired spectacularly and helps to explain why France and Britain were both so ready to work together in 1914. It also shows how Europe, at the start of the twentieth century, was a powder keg ready to be ignited.

78. The First World War Could Have Been Avoided

The assassination of the Archduke Franz Ferdinand is seen as the start of the countdown to war, but there was a genuine desire, on the part of many, to avoid just that. This period become known as 'the July Crisis'. Within two days of the assassination, Austro-Hungary correctly pointed the finger of blame at Serbia and demanded its cooperation in the investigation.

There was a debate about how to proceed. The initial plan was to mobilise against Serbia, but it was agreed that the general public should be prepared. This was bolstered by a letter from the kaiser on 5 July, referred to as Germany's 'blank cheque', in support of Austro-Hungary.

On 28 July the Austro-Hungarians presented their ten point ultimatum to Serbia. The plan was intended to humiliate and designed to be rejected. Confronted with this ultimatum and the lack of support from any European powers other than Russia, the Serbian cabinet felt it had no choice but to attempt a compromise. Unexpectedly, they agreed to eight of the ten points, which led to an intense diplomatic effort by the French and British to persuade Austro-Hungary to accept what was on offer. The ultimatum, which had been designed to provoke war, was now one step away from being a peace deal.

On 23 July the British Foreign Secretary, Sir Edward Grey, mediated an offer, but the diplomatic channels were sluggish and behind events as they were unfolding on the ground. So while Grey's idea was a good one and another chance to de-escalate the situation, he was unable to pull all the disparate parts together quickly enough. As it was, it had taken weeks to progress this far towards some kind of resolution.

On 25 July the Emperor Franz Joseph signed the mobilisation order to begin operations against Serbia. The next day German General von Moltke sent a message to Belgium demanding that German troops be allowed to pass through that kingdom.

To counter this, on the 27th, Grey sent another peace proposal, this time asking Germany to use its influence on Austria-Hungary. Grey warned that if Austria continued with its aggression towards Serbia and if Germany continued with its policy of support for Austria, then Britain would have no choice but to side with France and Russia.

The next day Austro-Hungary declared war on Serbia. On 30 July Tsar Nicholas sent a message to the kaiser informing him that he had ordered a partial mobilisation of Russian forces against Austria, not to antagonise Germany, but for Russia to show support for their Serbian allies. It didn't work. Germany threatened mobilisation if Russia did not demobilise at once. On 1 August, Germany declared war on Russia and the next day invaded Luxembourg (as it anticipated another war with France).

A few days later, Britain and France had joined as belligerents.

79. The British Had a Real Indiana Jones

If you visit the Natural History Museum in London and walk past the massive dinosaur towards the back of the main hall, you will see a statue of Charles Darwin at the top of the steps. To the left there's a bust of what looks like a hunter with a rifle. This is Frederick Selous, a fascinating man.

Born in 1851, Selous was one of five children from a wealthy aristocratic family (his father had been chairman of the London Stock Exchange). From a young age, it was obvious that Frederick was never going to be happy with a desk job – he had a burning desire to be an explorer. He enjoyed collecting birds' eggs and other native specimens, but the lure of faraway places beckoned. In the 1870s and 1880s, at the height of Victorian Britain, British armies, expeditions and explorers were travelling the world; Selous intended to be part of that.

Young Selous began his career by hunting game in what is now Zimbabwe. From then until 1890, with a few brief intervals in England, Selous explored the then little-known regions north of the Transvaal and south of the Congo Basin, befriending local tribesmen, shooting elephants and collecting some 5,000 plant and animal specimens for museums and private collections. It is counter-intuitive to us today that a man who hunted elephants should be in the Natural History Museum, but it was the fashion of the times to kill an animal and have it stuffed and mounted so that these recently discovered exotic species could be put on public display. Although he probably enjoyed the hunt, Selous was also concerned with the study and conservation of these new life forms, and his contributions greatly improved both scientific and cartographic understandings of south-east Africa.

Selous wrote about his adventures in a number of dynamic autobiographies, and his books were extremely popular, all of which added to his reputation as a 'great white hunter'. Indeed, he could count as friends Theodore Roosevelt and Cecil Rhodes, both of whom had similar reputations. In 1885 H. Rider Haggard wrote the action adventure novel *King Solomon's Mines* whose hero, Allan Quatermain, was inspired by Selous and his larger-than-life adventures.

Selous never stopped exploring. He was well into his sixties when the First World War broke out, and he enlisted in the 25th (Frontiersmen) Battalion, Royal Fusiliers. He may have been an atypical British subject, but his patriotism and desire to serve were quite common, a fact about the First World War that is largely forgotten today. He showed bravery and gallantry in East Africa, where he served throughout the war (a reminder that not all the fighting happened in Europe). He was killed by a sniper in 1917, age sixty-five.

Allan Quartermain was one of the models for the character of Indiana Jones, so if you visit the Natural History Museum, you might want to pay a visit to the man who helped to inspire it all.

80. 'The Sick Man of Europe' Humbled an Empire in Its Prime

The Ottoman Empire began in the late thirteenth century, a time when the Crusades were still a going concern. It reached its pinnacle in the sixteenth and seventeenth centuries, but by the start of the twentieth century, it was on its last legs and had been referred to as 'the sick man of Europe' for about a century.

As its empire had been slowly eaten away by Russia, Britain and France, the Ottomans joined the Germans in the First World War. It wasn't that the Germans and Ottomans were natural allies, more a case of 'my enemy's enemy is my friend'. The Ottoman capital city of Istanbul was on the very edge of the empire, and the Allies decided that, as Europe hunkered down to a trench warfare stalemate, they should deliver a fatal blow with an amphibious landing near the capital.

The Admiralty, under Winston Churchill, devised a plan to sail a fleet to the Dardanelles, where it would land tens of thousands of British and French troops, who would sweep inland to Istanbul. It wasn't a bad idea. A reasonable amount of planning and a sizeable number of troops were put into it; however, the Battle of Gallipoli was a disaster.

The factors were twofold: first of all, the reconnaissance of the landing zones wasn't thorough enough. When some of the troops went inland, they discovered that they had to scale cliffs where the Ottoman forces were waiting with machine guns. Secondly, those troops that did break inland were more concerned with regrouping than pushing on. Their failure to act quickly gave the Ottoman forces time to recover and fiercely resist.

Although the campaign has become forever associated with the Australian and New Zealand forces (Anzacs fighting in support of the motherland), there were always more British and French troops fighting on the ground. However, the first landings on 25 April 1915 are now commemorated in both Australia and New Zealand as Anzac Day, the most important national holiday honouring their military veterans and casualties.

For the Turks this battle was a matter of survival. If the Allies succeeded, they would carve up what remained of the Ottoman Empire, an unthinkable situation for their military leader, Mustafa Kemal. Sheer determination to win, at any cost, drove the man who emerged as Turkey's saviour, the man who would become the first president of the Republic of Turkey.

Regardless of nationality, all fought bravely. The British kept bringing more troops into the mix, hoping for a breakthrough. After eight months and a quarter of a million casualties, the Allies retreated in early January of 1916.

While Kemal went on to become known as 'Ataturk', the father of the Turks, Winston Churchill resigned from the Admiralty and joined the troops in the trenches to show his guilt and remorse for the Gallipoli debacle. The 'sick man' had protected its capital and repelled an empire in its prime.

81. Nobody and Everybody Won the Battle of Jutland

The German navy had been built in the 1870s, specifically to challenge the Royal Navy's superiority, but by 1916 there had been only a few inconclusive skirmishes between the two. In fact, the Royal Navy had seen no serious threat to its dominance since the time of Nelson more than a century earlier. That was in the era of sail and cannon, not steel and steam. Both sides were itching for a decisive showdown.

The opportunity came in late May of 1916. The Germans had assembled a mighty fleet with ninety-nine warships, including sixteen battleships. The British had even more, with 151 warships, including twenty-eight battleships, as well as one of the first aircraft carriers. The stage was set for a titanic clash at the Battle of Jutland.

The German plan was to use Vice-Admiral Franz Hipper's fast warships to lure Vice-Admiral Sir David Beatty's fleet into the path of the main German taskforce, where they would be annihilated by conventional warships on the surface and submarines from below. Although Beatty fell for the trap, the submarines weren't in position and played no part in the battle. That miscalculation, plus the arrival of British Admiral Sir John Jellicoe with the High Seas Fleet far faster than the Germans had anticipated, meant that the German plan was scuppered.

In this first brutal encounter twenty-five warships were sunk, killing thousands. Jellicoe wanted to ensure that the battle would be decisive and as dusk turned to night, tried to get behind the German fleet to stop it from heading for harbour. However, the Germans broke through and launched a final fan of torpedoes at the British fleet, hitting multiple ships before gaining the safety of port.

By the end of the battle, the British had lost fourteen ships and over 6,000 men, while the Germans lost eleven (mainly smaller) ships and over 2,000 men. There followed a raging debate as to who had won. The Germans claimed it was their victory because, according to every statistic, the British had come off worse. However, the German plan was not only to best the Royal Navy, but also to achieve dominance over the North Sea; yet after the battle, the German fleet was bottled up in port and never went anywhere for the rest of the war.

Instead, the Germans turned to unrestricted submarine warfare, sinking anything they could in the Atlantic, including civilian cruise liners. These disgraceful actions led to international condemnation, particularly after the sinking of the *Lusitania*, which had hundreds of Americans on board (the USA was a neutral country at the time).

Jellicoe and Beatty were not regarded as heroes of the Royal Navy and received no praise for their actions in the engagement. This rather inconclusive battle was no Trafalgar or Quiberon Bay. Despite the fact that these events happened in 1916, exactly who won the Battle of Jutland is still being debated today.

82. The Battle of the Somme Was Not a Defeat

A month after the Battle of Jutland the British Army was involved in the biggest bloodbath in its history; in fact, it was probably the biggest bloodbath in British history. Most people know that the British suffered 60,000 casualties on the first day at the Battle of the Somme. If that sounds bad, by the end of the campaign four months later, a million men had been killed or wounded. This was death on an industrial scale, so it may come as a surprise to learn that this was an Allied victory.

A primary reason for all the deaths was that imperial invention, the Maxim gun. By the summer of 1916 all the European powers had their variant, and as men tried to work their way through barbed wire (another Victorian invention), picking them off was like shooting fish in a barrel. These circumstances didn't even need machine guns as bolt-action rifles could also accurately fire dozens of shots over hundreds of meters. Some German soldiers stopped firing on that first day because they had had their fill of death.

The Battle of the Somme has been called the beginning of modern warfare, significant for its use of air power and the latest battlefield armaments. It was here that the British Army learned to fight the kind of mass-industrial war needed to win this attritional conflict.

Fought on both sides of the River Somme in France, the campaign dragged on for months largely due to the need to distract the Germans, who had been attacking the French around Verdun. France was being bled dry of fighting men and was in danger of collapse. The

Somme offensive was in no small part an attempt to take the pressure off Verdun and put pressure on the Germans.

Despite the battle's reputation for unprecedented casualties and long weeks of fighting, many areas in the Somme offensive (particularly in the French zone) were successfully captured on day one. By November, across most areas, the Allies had pushed the German troops back six miles into their own territory. It may not sound like much, but these were the biggest gains the Allies had made since 1914.

Meanwhile, the Germans had failed not only to break the French at Verdun, but also had suffered a substantial loss of territory and a staggering number of casualties at the Somme. In September of 1916, the Germans essentially admitted defeat when the high command decided to build a new fall-back line of fortifications. This was known to the Germans as the Siegfriedstellung and to the British as the Hindenburg Line. Here's a quote from one of the German high command about the effect on the German forces of the Somme campaign: 'What remained of the old first-class peace-trained German infantry had been expended on the battlefield.' The Somme was an Allied victory. It just didn't feel like one.

83. Imperial Invention No. 9: The Tank

Although the Somme was the scene of unbearable loss of life, it was also the first place an ingenious new invention saw action. It was designed to protect soldiers from withering enemy fire as they manoeuvred across no man's land, crossing ditches and cutting through barbed wire. Something like a steam roller was needed to do the job, so the British invented the tank.

Some credit Leonardo da Vinci and even H. G. Wells with early concepts of moving, armoured vehicles, but in reality, the idea needed the combustion engine, steel plating and continuous caterpillar tracks to work.

Originally called 'landships', the tank was initially a Royal Navy project. In order to conceal the true nature of these armour-clad machines, they had 'tank' written on them so spies would think they were mobile water carriers. After a year of tests, it was decided to produce two types of tank: 'male' tanks were armed with six-pound cannons and machine guns, while 'female' tanks didn't have the canons but were fitted with more machine guns.

They were first seen on the Somme on 1 September, when some German troops fled in terror as they saw their bullets bounce off the advancing armoured behemoths.

A forgotten British officer, J. F.C. Fuller, recognised the potential of tanks and went on to develop practical strategies for using them. His ideas influenced the Germans, who later used his ideas to fight a highly mobile kind of warfare they called 'Blitzkrieg'.

84. One Decoded Message Changed the Course of a War

It is rare that just one decoded message can change the course of a war, but in the case of the Zimmerman telegram, that's exactly what happened. At the start of the First World War Germany knew it needed as many allies as possible to avoid strategic encirclement. The Ottoman Empire joined the war on Germany's side in 1914, and from 1914–16 everything went surprisingly well. Then the Germans stirred trouble in Ireland; the 1916 Easter uprising was funded and equipped by them. Unfortunately for both Ireland and Germany, the uprising didn't last long, Britain prevailed, and Germany had to cast around for another way to distract the Allies. They struck gold with the 'sealed train' that took Lenin from exile back into Russia – the subsequent revolution would take Russia out of the European conflict in 1917. Emboldened by the success of this manoeuvre, the Germans apparently thought, 'Why not have another go?'

This time a coded message was sent from Herr Arthur Zimmermann, in the German government, to Mexico. The message offered favourable terms (including a return of territories in Arizona, New Mexico and Texas) and practical support if Mexico attacked America, which would prevent it from providing troops or playing any effective role on the Western Front. Not a bad idea, except Mexico had its own problems (namely a civil war) and was in no position to do anything about the offer.

As the death toll spiralled into the millions, the British continued their efforts to involve America in the war, but the US was not interested. Anti-Mexican, anti-British and anti-French almost as much as they were anti-German, the Americans were mostly anti-getting-into-the-war-in-Europe. Not even the sinking of the civilian cruise liner *Lusitania* by a German U-boat could provoke them into taking action. But Britain managed to intercept and decode the German message to Mexico. It was a clear act of war that the British showed to the US government. The message suggested such a blatant act of aggression and was so outrageous in its content that many in the US government dismissed it as a British forgery. Step forward Arthur Zimmerman, who made one of the worst decisions in history. America was ready to believe Zimmerman if he said it was all a British trick. The result would be a further rift between the US and Britain, and Germany would not create a fresh, recently industrialised enemy.

In March of 1917, a press conference was called, and Zimmerman came clean, admitting that the message was genuine. The Germans had been targeting both passenger and merchant ships with American flags since February, but once Zimmerman's announcement was made public, US popular opinion demanded action. Finally in April, the American government declared war on Germany. Zimmerman not only made one of the biggest tactical mistakes in history, but he also holds the record for the worst outcome from a press conference.

85. THE FIRST WORLD WAR ENDED IN DECISIVE VICTORY

The Battle of Amiens, which started on 8 August 1918, marked a period when the German forces were consistently pushed back for three months. This later became known as the 'Hundred Days', one of the longest periods of continual success in British military history. It is also a reminder that the First World War did not end in a stalemate but in a decisive victory for the British Empire and France.

Contrary to the popular misconception that nothing changed on the Western Front, the Battle of Amiens showed how modern the British Army had become in four years. Backed by a precision artillery barrage, 500 tanks rolled into battle. Planes flew overhead in support of the tanks and the infantry, which used the tanks as protection from the German fire. Some of the British soldiers were armed with Lewis guns, a more mobile version of the machine gun (ironically, another machine gun designed by an American but used by the British).

The initial assault had been carefully concealed from the Germans. On the first day, more than 30,000 Germans were killed or wounded, 17,000 were captured and 330 field guns were taken, making this an unqualified success. A few weeks later the British tried another offensive in the Somme. This one pushed the German troops back over thirty miles. The German Hindenburg line was breached in September.

Amiens was one of the first major battles involving tanks, so the Allies, in effect, had already won the battle of mobility. This development also marked the end of trench warfare on the Western Front. Week after week, German troops either surrendered or were forced to give up territory they had held since 1914. The hasty retreats meant that much of the German heavy equipment fell into the hands of the Allies not only further reducing Germany's ability to fight but also enabling the Allies to use German equipment against German troops.

The speed of the collapse meant everyone knew the end was near, which also meant that the huge Allied offensive, scheduled for 1919, thankfully, could be shelved.

By October of 1918, a string of successes and the obvious collapse of German offensive capabilities prompted telegrams from the German high command to the American government requesting an armistice. All the forces involved agreed that this should come into effect on the eleventh hour, of the eleventh day, of the eleventh month.

The last casualty of the war was a twenty-three-year-old American private, Henry Gunther, of German-American heritage. Troubled by conflicting loyalties, Gunther did not enlist but was drafted. When he wrote home about the 'miserable conditions' on the front, he was demoted. Bitter but now obsessed with proving his worth, he disobeyed orders and charged a German unit with his bayonet. He was killed at 10.59 on 11 November by stunned German soldiers who were aware that the Armistice was imminent and had tried, unsuccessfully, to wave him off.

86. THE SUFFRAGETTES WERE FEMALE TERRORISTS

The fact that women should have the right to vote is, in today's parlance, a 'no brainer'. The stark segregation of women's rights is an alien concept in modern British society. However, barely 100 years ago, British women were willing to do anything to be heard by the male politicians of the time. These outspoken campaigners had moral right on their side, but that's not to say everything they did was morally right.

The movement for women's suffrage started in the late nineteenth century when Millicent Fawcett organised peaceful protests in support of votes for women. She believed that any violence would only undermine the cause, so she and her followers worked long and patiently – and achieved very little.

Political inaction led to frustration, and in 1903, Emmeline Pankhurst and her daughters founded the Women's Social and Political Union. Known as 'suffragettes', they wanted the right to vote NOW, and they were prepared to use violence to achieve it. Early peaceful demonstrations led to noisy disruptions at political gatherings where the suffragettes were abused and arrested. They refused to pay their fines and were happy to go to prison, where many embarked on hunger strikes.

On 21 June 1908, 500,000 activists rallied in Hyde Park to demand votes for women. Surely Prime Minister Asquith would not ignore this powerful message ... but he did. Lack of political recognition for their cause led to ever more extreme acts on the part of the suffragettes who burned down churches, vandalised Oxford Street, attacked politicians and fire-bombed their homes. They chained themselves to the rails at Buckingham Palace and hired boats, sailed up the Thames and shouted abuse through loud hailers at Parliament. Most famously, Emily Davison died when she threw herself under the king's horse, and the suffragettes had their first martyr.

Fighting for their rights was one thing, but life-threatening violence was another, and these acts met with understandable widespread condemnation.

It was the First World War that did the suffragettes a favour. With millions of men away fighting, someone had to do the 'men's work' back in Britain. Pankhurst called a halt to the violence and urged women to support the government in the war effort. The First World War was a total war, where everyone had to do their bit, and the women of Britain stepped up to keep the country going.

As a result, the Representation of the People Act 1918 was passed, enfranchising women over the age of thirty if they met minimum property qualifications. This gave the right to vote to over 8 million women for the first time. It was followed up nine months later with the Eligibility of Women Act, allowing women to become MPs. Finally, the Representation of the People Act 1928 gave the vote to all women over the age of twenty-one. For the first time in British history every adult (of 'sound mind' and not in prison) had the right to vote. Britain was at last a modern democracy.

87. THE BBC FEARED ADVERTISING WOULD LOWER STANDARDS

It is a strange fact that if you want to own a TV in Britain, you have to have a licence. Failure to buy one can lead to a large fine or even imprisonment. The reason for this is that Britain has had, almost since its inception, a publically funded broadcaster called the British Broadcasting Corporation, known universally by its initials, the BBC.

Founded in 1922, the BBC's main responsibility is to provide impartial public service broadcasting. It is the oldest and largest national broadcasting system in the world. Fearing that paid advertising would lower standards, just a year into its existence, the powers-that-be decided that the BBC should be funded by means of a licence fee, originally set at ten shillings (about £65 in today's money).

By 1932 the BBC had introduced the Empire Service, later called the World Service, an invaluable radio broadcaster that could be picked up almost anywhere in the world, thanks to the imperial network of radio transmitters.

In 1934 the BBC was first in the world to experiment with television. By 1936 this had been enhanced to an electronic form of TV broadcasting, but further developments came to a halt with the outbreak of the Second World War. However, it's remarkable to think that Bruce Forsyth, still performing in the era of satellite and HD TV, first performed on television in 1939 on one of the most literally named TV shows ever created: *Come and be Televised*.

88. IMPERIAL INVENTION No. 10: TV

The town of Hastings has made two contributions to history; it was the site of a famous battle in 1066, and in 1923, a Scottish engineer called John Logie Baird invented television. Although the development of television was the result of work by many inventors, Baird was a key pioneer who, over the years, made major contributions to the field.

Baird was recuperating from poor health in Hastings when he decided to pass his time by tinkering with an old tea chest, a hat box pierced by darning needles, scissors and some bicycle light lenses, all held together with sealing wax and glue. This was the birth of the television.

This first TV was a mechanical, low-definition device, first publically demonstrated in Selfridges in 1925. By 1927 Baird was able to broadcast his moving images from London to Glasgow, and the picture quality had improved from 5 to 12.5 frames per second. From 1929–1937 the BBC experimented with TV broadcasting, but it was obvious that Baird's mechanical system had severe limitations.

In the meantime, an electronic version of television had been created in America. This is the system on which modern television is based and why some claim that TV was invented in America. Even though this system was undeniably better, it is worth pointing out that the electronic format was then still theoretical, little more than a collection of designs, while Baird's TV system was already broadcasting up and down the country.

89. ERNEST RUTHERFORD WAS A REAL ALCHEMIST

Ernest Rutherford was a child of the empire. His mother was from Essex, and his father was from Scotland. They emigrated to New Zealand where Ernest was born. Like all New Zealand men (allegedly), he played rugby and went to the University of New Zealand (in his case, to study physics). From there he travelled to Britain for post graduate work, thus making the whole emigration thing somewhat pointless. He spent a large part of his academic career at McGill University in Canada, later returning to England where he was chair of physics at Manchester University.

Rutherford was a genius, drawn to that small and mysterious world of the atom. His extensive experimental work on alpha radiation won him the Nobel Prize for Chemistry in 1908, which shows how the two disciplines blurred into each other at the time. (At no point did all of this tinkering with radiation turn him into a superhero.)

But it didn't end there. Rutherford also correctly hypothesised that atoms come with a charge and created the Rutherford model of the atom in 1911, which was vital to the understanding of atomic structure. During the First World War he turned his gigantic intellect to helping the war effort. He was particularly interested in devising a way to detect enemy submarines, but he couldn't crack it. However, it was also during the war that he conducted his most famous 'gold foil' experiment.

As this is a light-hearted history book and not a physics textbook, I'll hit the highlights and generalise. In essence what Rutherford did was to pass subatomic particles through a sheet of gold foil. This led to several remarkable discoveries. Perhaps most significantly, he was the first person in history to deliberately change one element into another (in this instance, nitrogen to oxygen). This meant that he was also the first person to split an atom. Some of his earlier results had pointed to science's then incomplete understanding of atomic structure, but it was this experiment that proved the existence of protons, which Rutherford named.

Working with the famous physicist Niels Bohr in 1921, Rutherford theorised the existence of neutrons. It would take more than a decade to prove, but Rutherford's associate, James Chadwick, confirmed their existence and won the Nobel Prize in 1935.

It is difficult to over-estimate the importance of Rutherford's work, which established (among other things) the nuclear structure of the atom and the essential nature of radioactive decay as a nuclear process. It is because of all this that he is considered to be the father of nuclear physics. He was knighted in 1914 and raised to the peerage as Baron Rutherford of Nelson in 1931. After his death in 1937, he was honoured by being interred with the greatest scientists of the United Kingdom, near Sir Isaac Newton's tomb in Westminster Abbey. In 1997 he received the posthumous honour of having an exotic element named after him: Rutherfordium (Rf, atomic number 104).

90. NOT MANY MEN CALLED FRANK MAKE HISTORY

If there's one thing the British can produce, it's a boffin, a scientific eccentric who can create something practical from the most unlikely of sources. John Logie Baird was one example and Frank Whittle is another.

Although the convention in history books is to refer to someone by surname, there just aren't that many people called Frank making history, so to honour this rare example, I'll be using Frank's first name to tell his story.

Frank was an excellent engineer and decided to join the one organisation that was always thinking ahead, the Royal Air Force (created in the First World War, the RAF is the oldest air force in the world). He became an excellent pilot and, later, test pilot and particularly enjoyed flying his Bristol Fighter and performing all kinds of aerobatic tricks.

In 1927, as part of his officer training, he was required to write a thesis. His chosen subject was *Future Developments in Aircraft Design*, and it was this that put him in the history books. Frank came up with the concept of a 'motor jet'. The idea was a bit hazy to start with, but he persisted until eventually, in 1930, he took out a patent for his turbojet engine.

That's right. Nearly ten years before the Second World War the RAF had the designs for a jet engine, an engine that would make aircraft substantially faster and able to fly at much higher altitudes than any propeller driven aircraft.

Frank's performance in his training course was so exceptional that in 1934 he was released to study engineering at Cambridge, but it was while he was there that his patent came up for renewal, and unable to fund the £5 fee, the patent lapsed, making it available to anyone in the world.

Following Cambridge, Frank was given the funds to develop his invention, and by 1937 he had a working prototype. But it turned out that the RAF wasn't quite as forward thinking as Frank had expected, and the whole project was treated as an oddity. Up until this point the Germans had been consistently behind the British in terms of jet engine development, but while Frank only had a working engine, the Germans had their first prototype test flight in 1938.

It was government indifference and poor organisation that meant that the Battle of Britain was fought with propeller craft and not a fleet of jet fighters that would have annihilated the Luftwaffe. As it was, the first British prototype jetfighter didn't take off until 1941 – and not before Frank had suffered a nervous breakdown because of all the stress and frustration.

In some ways the story of the jet engine is a microcosm of the rot that had begun to seep into the British Empire. 100 years earlier, people like Brunel were able to get huge amounts of funding for their high concept ideas. By the 1930s, innovative ideas were all too frequently being stifled by bureaucracy.

91. WINSTON CHURCHILL WAS A PRISONER, DRINKER, WIT, HERO AND LEGEND

If Sir Francis Drake personified the early era of empire and Nelson the middle, then Churchill (born in 1874) is the obvious choice to symbolise the late imperial age.

Churchill has already cropped up in earlier facts. He was in the last great imperial cavalry charge at Omdurman. He was a prisoner of war (before escaping) in the Boer War. He was the First Lord of the Admiralty in the First World War, and after his plan at Gallipoli failed, he resigned and joined the troops in the trenches – a remarkable act of contrition.

Churchill returned to government before the end of the First World War and went on to write one of its definitive histories. In his own words, 'History will be kind to me, as I intend to write it.' All of this occurred before his 'finest hour'.

By the mid-1930s Churchill was in his early sixties, and, quite frankly, his best years should have been behind him. His grumbles about imperial decline, troublemakers like Gandhi and the threat from Hitler were largely ignored. However, by May of 1940, after Britain had declared war on Germany and things were heating up on the continent, it became apparent that Neville Chamberlain was leading the country to disaster. In the event, Chamberlain resigned and Churchill became prime minister – and war leader. His belligerence, his never-say-die intransigence and his exceptional speech craft inspired and rallied war-weary Brits and were as vital as the RAF in saving the nation.

Churchill came to symbolise Britain in the Second World War, and yet he was not the country's leader at the end of it. In the summer of 1945 he lost the general election, leading Conservative politicians today to remark (something like), 'Who cares about our legacy; if Churchill can win a war and lose an election, we mustn't take anything for granted.'

Churchill was well known for his 'dependence' on alcohol, although it would appear that his fondness for whiskey was at least partly a prop – like his cigars – which were allowed to go out and usually discarded after being well chewed. While he had a formidable capacity, he was known to dislike drunkards, commenting that a glass of champagne lifts the spirits and sharpens the wits, but 'a bottle produces the opposite effect'.

In 1951, at the age of seventy-seven, Churchill became prime minister once again. In this final era, partially defined by nuclear proliferation, he coined the term 'iron curtain', which came to summarise the ideological and physical boundaries between East and West from the end of the Second World War until the end of the Cold War in 1991. Churchill's career started with cavalry charges and ended with nuclear weapons – an extraordinary span. On his death in 1965 he was given a state funeral, and the world's leaders came to pay their respects to a man who was universally recognised as one of the greatest leaders of the age.

92. It's Not Carrots that Make You See in the Dark

It wasn't just Churchill and the brave fighter pilots of the RAF who won the Battle of Britain; a new development was also critical to that success.

The discovery of radar (an acronym from RAdio Detection And Ranging) has multiple parents. By the twentieth century, radio experiments were taking place in many laboratories in many parts of the world. However, the first practical radar system was developed by Robert Watson-Watt (another Scot who made his career in England) just in time for the outbreak of the Second World War.

By the late 1930s every nation understood the danger of fast attack planes. To counter this, many countries had bizarre sound amplification devices, like giant stethoscopes, in an attempt to detect the noise of aircraft engines from far away. It sort of worked, but radar was superior in every possible way and was one of Britain's secret weapons during the war.

Radar works by emitting radio waves from a fixed point. If they hit the surface of (say) an airplane, they are distorted or bounce back. Either way, an observer looking at the flow of the radio waves will see the disruptions as they appear on a screen. Keep firing the waves at the aircraft, and it is possible to determine its speed and direction. This was vital in getting squadrons of Spitfires and Hurricanes to the places where they could do the most damage, before they needed to be refuelled.

Radar was vital in concentrating the RAF's firepower against wave after wave of Luftwaffe planes as the Germans attacked the south of England. This is why there are pictures of fighter pilots sitting in full flight gear in armchairs next to their planes. Radar could detect enemy aircraft far enough out to give the fighter squadrons time to get airborne, get into formation and position themselves ready for attack.

The British high command realised the Germans would probably deduce that all these interceptions weren't blind luck. So, to protect the secret of radar, they started producing propaganda to mislead the Germans. The reason for all this success? Carrots. Apparently the RAF had been feeding its crews with carrots because it was a 'scientific fact' that carrots improve eye sight. The bluff worked, and the Germans actually carried out experiments that involved feeding its pilots with carrots ... lots and lots of carrots. Unsurprisingly, the German tests didn't have the desired effect, but the secret of radar was safe.

93. THE PEOPLE AT STATION X WERE THE MOST IMPORTANT CODE BREAKERS IN HISTORY

Britain's best kept secret of the Second World War was so important and so secret that until a book came out in 1974, no one in the wider world knew anything about it. Of the thousands of people who worked on the site, not a single person broke ranks. Churchill referred to the code breakers as 'the geese that laid the golden eggs and never cackled'. It wasn't until the 1990s that the general public became interested in the story of Station X, better known today as Bletchley Park.

During the First World War, Germany felt safe in the knowledge that its new code machines (called Enigma) could scramble a message in 100,391,791,500 ways. Just to be safe, they increased the encryption to 150,738,274,937,250. And just to make triply sure, the codes were changed EVERY day.

However, the British (with the help of Polish spies) were reading the apparently unbreakable codes within months of war breaking out. The flaw in the codes was simply that machines cannot be random, so there will be a pattern, no matter how well hidden. Also, operators make mistakes, and any time a message is repeated, it leaves a clue about how the encryption works.

It was all very clever stuff, but re-cracking the codes every day was arduous and exhausting. So a young maths genius called Alan Turing devised a mechanical system to help speed up the process. He called his devices 'bombes', but in 1943 these rudimentary machines were the size of rooms. The largest of these was called 'Colossus', and because it could be primed or, in other words, 'programmed', it represented a major leap forwards. In essence what Turing had done was to invent the world's first programmable computer.

Although Turing is now regarded as the father of modern computing, it is ironic that his successes were so secret nobody knew about them, which meant that when computers were invented later, their development was independent of his work.

Because Turing was gay, this troubled genius was treated abysmally by his own government, and, after the war, was considered to be a major security risk. In 1952, when it was still a crime, Turing was tried for homosexuality. Faced with imprisonment or chemical castration, he chose the latter, underwent hormone therapy and grew small breasts. This timid but brilliant man is said to have committed suicide by eating an apple laced with cyanide, but the apple was not tested, and his family maintained it was an accident caused by his careless storage of chemicals. Either way, it was a tragic ending to the life of a remarkable pioneer.

Many events are said to be 'game changers', but on closer inspection, most are not. However, there can be no doubt that while it was likely the Allies were going to win the war, work on cracking the German codes shortened the conflict by at least two years – and saved hundreds of thousands of lives.

94. A DESERT FOX WAS BEATEN BY DESERT RATS

The German Field Marshal Erwin Rommel put the fear of God into British troops. He was regarded as a brilliant tactician … and invincible. British forces had suffered multiple defeats at the hands of his Afrika Korps, which included the dreaded Panzer tank divisions. Even Tobruk, which had repelled an early assault, eventually crumbled when Rommel returned. He was given the nickname 'Desert Fox' for his cunning and speedy strikes.

But by late 1942 Rommel found himself at the end of a long supply line near the Egyptian border. It was here that he faced a new British general, the flamboyant Bernard 'Monty' Montgomery, who had chosen his stand well. Thanks to Montgomery's position and the geography near El Alamein, Rommel would have to face Montgomery in a head-on collision. More than anything, Montgomery wanted to ensure victory. A defeat here would mean Rommel would be able to march into Egypt, capture the Suez Canal and head to the oilfields of the Middle East (the Third Reich desperately needed more oil). On a personal note, it would also mean the end of Montgomery's career.

So, rather than do anything risky, Montgomery was eminently sensible. In the inevitable slugging match to come, he made sure he had more of everything. He had over 50 per cent more troops and double the numbers of tanks and artillery. The only arena in which the two sides were even roughly matched was aircraft. Additionally, Monty made it seem as if he would attack from a different position than the one he had planned. Among Montgomery's massed army of

THE BRITISH EMPIRE IN 100 FACTS

179

nearly 200,000 was the British 7th Armoured Division. Known as the 'Desert Rats', they had been fighting in many of the North African campaigns and were now experienced in desert warfare.

The battle started with an almighty artillery barrage as more than 500,000 shells were fired over the entire forty-mile front in the first few hours. Then Montgomery's sappers moved into no man's land to start clearing mines so the tanks could attack. It was all rather reminiscent of the First World War, except with much faster armour and a lot more sand.

The fighting lasted more than two weeks, but by then end of it, Rommel had lost around half of his men (killed, wounded or captured) and, most critically, about 90 per cent of his tanks. Rommel had no option but to retreat, but where to? He was literally in the middle of nowhere. What followed was one of the longest but fastest retreats in history as the Desert Fox was chased out of Africa by the Desert Rats and Montgomery's 8th Army, which harassed Rommel the entire way. This victory marked a turning point in the war, particularly in North Africa.

It was just after this that Churchill made his famous observation, 'It is not the end, nor even the beginning of the end, but it is the end of the beginning.'

95. British Ingenuity Can Be Devastating

The Second World War can be considered a golden age for British boffins. Radar, computers and jet engines were all the works of geniuses allowed to run riot with their imaginations. Another of these genius boffins was Barnes Wallace.

In 1943 it was thought that a strategic strike on the German industrial heartland would slow the German war effort. The targets were three dams in the Ruhr valley. The problem (apart from their location in the heart of the Third Reich and their heavy defences provided by anti-aircraft emplacements and fighter interceptors) was how to damage a dam. Most dams at this time had protective nets around them, so torpedoes were not an option.

Wallace's original notion was a bomb that would skip along the surface of the water, but as that would only clip the edge of the dam, causing minimal damage, he came up with the genius idea of the 'bouncing bomb'. Because of its spin (it was cylindrical rather than spherical) it would hit the side of the dam, spin down the wall and detonate deep below the water line, causing catastrophic damage to the dam wall.

The RAF operation was not called 'Dam Busters', but the far calmer Operation Chastise. In order to succeed, the Lancaster bombers needed to fly low not only to avoid German radar, but also for the bombs to work effectively. Of the nineteen planes that flew the mission, eight were shot down and fifty-three airmen were killed. Although two dams were successfully breached, Wallace always questioned whether the results justified the losses. But the disruption of hydro-electric power devastated German industry, and it was estimated that coal production dropped by 400,000 tons in the following months. Because this had been an unexpected strike at their very centre, the damage to the Germans was psychological as well as physical.

But Wallace wasn't finished with his ingenious munitions. He also created an 'earthquake bomb'. This was a massive steel-tipped explosive that only detonated underground, causing significant amounts of collateral damage. It was decided to use a variant of this on one of Germany's most formidable weapons.

The battleship *Tirpitz* was the sister ship of the *Bismarck,* and both had been responsible for huge amounts of loss and damage when they roamed the Atlantic. However, while the RAF was losing valuable planes and men trying to destroy it, the *Tirpitz* was very successfully being protected in a fjord in Norway. And like the dams, it was also protected by torpedo netting. A direct hit by a bomb was called for.

Eventually, in November 1944, the RAF launched Operation Catechism. Thirty Lancaster bombers, each armed with a five-ton bomb called a Tallboy, attacked the *Tirpitz*. Once again Wallace's ingenious device did the trick and the ship capsized, killing 1,000 of the 1,900 men on board.

Although Wallace's legacy is more about destruction than that of some of the other boffins, it doesn't make his contributions any less momentous.

96. IN WINNING A WAR, BRITAIN LOST AN EMPIRE

Britain is the only major power to have fought from the start to the end of the Second World War, and the country can be justifiably proud of its vital contribution.

But Britain did not 'win' the war; it was on the winning side, and that's an important difference. By the end of the conflict two other powers had gained the most from the spoils of war: the Union of Soviet Socialist Republics and the United States of America. The USSR absorbed vast areas of Eastern Europe, while the USA became the dominant global power. Their gains had to be at the expense of another power, in this case, the British Empire, the end of which started in 1945, according to some historians (there are three more 'ends of the empire' discussed later).

By 1945 Britain had called in all its favours and spent all its resources resisting its greatest-ever threat. If the idea that an empire could be bankrupt after winning a war seems odd today, it seemed even odder back then. The situation was so desperate that Britain sent its Nobel Prize winning economist, John Maynard Keynes, to Washington to explain why the world's largest empire needed emergency loans from a nation it once owned. The loan he managed to negotiate saved Britain from starving. Keynes is remembered as a great economist, but he may be the only economist who saved lives.

97. OLD INDIA BECOMES THREE DIFFERENT COUNTRIES

Although the Second World War is frequently used to signal the end of the British Empire, events two years later also played a significant part. It is astonishing that the last few decades of empire were not marked by a maelstrom of nasty colonial wars in which Britain tried to cling on to its dominions through increased brutality. Sound farfetched? Look no further than the contemporary empire of the French, which disintegrated in brutal fighting in French-Indochina (Vietnam) and Algeria.

Britain had always, with great admiration, looked to the Roman Empire ... which was ironic as they were fundamentally different enterprises. The Roman Empire (in the West) slowly imploded over two or three generations as wave after wave of militant immigrants smashed their way in. The last emperor was a boy who was quietly deposed, bringing the empire to an end. Even as endings go, it was all pretty depressing.

By the twentieth century, Britain was aware that all empires come to an end and began to allow dominions, like Canada and Australia, to self-govern in the framework of a commonwealth, a construct of empire where lands and peoples were allowed to leave ... if they asked nicely.

By far the biggest undertaking was the independence of India in 1947. When independence began to look like a certainty, the Muslim communities of India demanded self-rule as they didn't want to be governed by the Hindu majority. So the authorities worked out a plan that looked great on paper but was a nightmare in reality. India was to be split into two countries: the

Hindu India, and to the north-west and east, Muslim Pakistan. The name Pakistan is an acronym using the letters of the lands it covers: Punjab, North-West Frontier Province (Afghania Province), Kashmir, Sindh, and Baluchistan.

Of course, the Muslim population of India was spread across the sub-continent, so for the plan to work, millions had to move (including Hindus in the newly created Muslim Pakistan). The division led to the largest mass migration in history as 10 million people crossed the various borders. The movement also enflamed sectarian passions, and it is estimated 1.5 million people were killed in the process (both through violence and accidents). To be clear, these weren't British soldiers massacring locals, this was people from India and Pakistan, who up until that point had all been part of the same country, slaughtering each other. Gandhi's drive for independence had been won by means of non-violent protest, so it was nothing short of tragic that his peaceful legacy should backfire in this way.

India had been the 'jewel in the crown' of the British Empire, and its loss was an obvious sign of the empire's demise. Pakistan ended up splitting itself into Pakistan and Bangladesh, and a number of wars have been fought between India and Pakistan, with an ongoing insurgency between Muslims and Hindus in Kashmir. What was messy then has repercussions today.

98. It's Not the Good Old Days Anymore

Since its creation in the nineteenth century, the Suez Canal had been a key artery in the British Empire, vital for access to the East. Although Britain had lost India, it still had territories in Asia and needed the canal for the flow of oil. It therefore came as a terrible shock when, in July of 1956, the new President of Egypt, Gamal Abdel Nasser, declared the Suez Canal to be the national asset of Egypt. If he blocked Britain's right of use, the move would cripple the British economy. It was a red rag to a bull, and Britain was determined not to let an anti-imperialist upstart get away with it.

By this time, Churchill had finally retired from politics, and a new, more dynamic prime minister had taken his place. Anthony Eden was seen as the poster boy for a new generation of British politicians – great things were expected of him. When it came to a showdown over Suez, Eden allied with the French and the new country of Israel to carry out a daring raid to humble the Egyptian army and reclaim the canal.

In the winter of 1957, the three allies were ready to attack. The combined force numbered 250,000 (mainly Israelis), against an Egyptian national army of about 300,000. The assault was a complete success. The Suez Canal was recaptured, and the Egyptian military was humbled. Everything had pretty much gone to plan ... but then things started to unravel.

All of this had been carried out as it had been in 'the good old days'. While opinions had been canvassed throughout the Commonwealth, there had been no attempt to get international backing. When US President Eisenhower heard of the invasion, he was furious. Such naked aggression by Western Europe would force Nasser to look for help from the Soviet Union. The prospect of the Suez Canal falling under Communist rule was unacceptable from an American perspective.

The United States was quick to react. Along with financial threats, the US publicly condemned the invasion of Egypt and started an oil embargo against Britain and France. Eden was forced to back down. A ceasefire was called, and the allied troops beat an ignominious retreat. It was a harsh lesson in how world politics had changed; Britain was no longer a world power and could not act with impunity.

Because this plan had been championed and led by Eden, he had nobody to blame but himself. The golden boy of politics was forced to resign over the Suez Crisis and is often referred to as the worst prime minister of the twentieth century. It is a sobering example of just how quickly the pendulum can swing for anyone in politics.

Ironically, years later, Eisenhower realised that his actions had actually damaged the West. Britain and France were humbled, and Egypt turned towards the Soviet Union anyway. Except for Nasser, the crisis had been a disaster for everyone.

99. The Malayan Emergency Was Definitely not a War

Picture the scene: dense rainforest, steep hills, dangerous wildlife, jungle foliage so dense you can barely see a metre in front of you – and you have to fight a war against communist guerrilla troops in this environment. The Vietnam War? No, the Malayan Emergency.

The reason why this war ... I mean emergency ... was so called was because of insurance. Insurers don't pay out in war zones, so to keep the economy safe, the conflict was never overtly referred to as a 'war', but a war it was in everything but name.

The Malayan Communist Party (MCP), backed by communist China, wanted better working conditions on rubber plantations, but their solution was to murder plantation owners. To help counteract the insurgency and end the slaughter, Malayan officials asked the British to stay on. In another sign that the end of the British Empire was different from others, this was a case where the locals wanted to continue the imperial relationship, at least for the foreseeable future. The British agreed, not because it would give them any long-term advantage, but because it was the right thing to do.

During the fighting, from 1948 to 1960, tens of thousands of British and Commonwealth soldiers fought valiantly for a country that was to become independent. It was in 1951 that the term 'winning hearts and minds' came into use. British counter-insurgency plans didn't just cover fighting in the jungles, but also made certain that locals received certain benefits, including medical care, from anti-communist groups so as to ensure a measure of loyalty. Over time, all of this worked.

As many members of the MCP were ethnic Chinese, it was decided to concentrate Chinese communities in areas where they could be kept under surveillance. An insurgency can't function effectively if infiltrators can't melt into the local population. Obviously armed troops could be easily spotted in the new settlements, and informants revealed communist plans to the authorities. Additionally, Britain used its jungle warfare experience (mainly in Burma) to mount ambushes. With the further involvement of elite units like the SAS, the insurgency gradually faded away. The MCP was no longer a cause worth fighting for, and the communist leaders were exiled.

This was not a clean war. Guerrillas hid among civilians, and when civilians and insurgents could not be differentiated, bloodbaths were inescapable. This conflict is inevitably compared to the Vietnam War (which started warming up almost as soon as this 'emergency' ended). Britain, which was in imperial decline, used all of its knowledge and experience gained through colonial wars in order to achieve victory. By comparison, America, in its military prime, was humbled in part because it hadn't bothered to learn from the experiences of others, notably the British in Malaya.

Malaya (now Malaysia) became independent in 1963. Ironically, because Singapore disagreed about some of the points of independence, it broke away to become its own (rather unexpected) country around the same time.

100. The Handover of Hong Kong Was the Last True Act of Empire

Congratulations, reader, on reaching the final fact in the book. Well done on sticking with it. It's been a long journey, so allow me to remind you of the very first date, all the way back in fact 1. Newfoundland was claimed for the English throne in 1497, marking the start of the British Empire. Wouldn't it be satisfying to have an event in 1997 that could mark a tidy end to empire? A nice, neat 500 years of British imperial history?

As luck would have it, there is! Hong King was returned to China in 1997. The territory had become part of the British Empire as a concession by the Chinese at the end of the Opium Wars. It's one of those places that flies in the face of the idea that 'empire' is automatically a dirty word with evil connotations. When the British took over the running of the area in 1841, it was nothing more than a few fishing villages; by the 1990s, it was one of the financial capitals of the world. With its deep natural harbour and a horizon made up of tightly packed skyscrapers, it has one of the densest populations in the world. Known as the Manhattan of the East, it was, in 1997, the richest city in China with one of the world's highest per capita incomes (but an enormous disparity in wealth). In the course of its history it generated billions of pounds for the British government, so while it was a small territory, it was hugely profitable ... a bit like the sugar-producing Caribbean islands in the eighteenth century.

Hong Kong's urban sprawl started in the mid-nineteenth century when the British founded the

'City of Victoria' (the tradition of unimaginative naming hadn't changed). The city was never abandoned; it just evolved into what there is today, a colony in which Britain had heavily invested. But the island was not owned by Britain; it was a leasehold property, and the lease ran out in 1997. Rather than fighting over it – or even trying to negotiate an extension – Britain honoured the original treaty, and the Crown colony was returned to China. Mindful of its responsibilities to the local population, the British insisted on certain stipulations to protect Hong Kong's inhabitants. It was agreed that the territory would be governed as a 'special administrative region' of China and would be semi-autonomous for at least fifty years.

Since the British left, mainland China has tried, gradually, to impose communist rule, but such governance is anathema to the locals, who are determined to resist. Now that the Beijing government is in charge, there is more civil unrest in Hong Kong than anything prior to 1997.

1497–1997: a score of 500. Using a cricket analogy (another great British invention that there just weren't enough facts for), that's not a bad innings.